"To Lisa Lyons Durkin . . . . with gratitude for her vision, encouragement, and support."

CONCEPT COOKERY

Learning Concepts Through Cooking

by
Kathy Faggella
Art by
Debby Dixler

FIRST TEACHER PRESS
First Teacher, Inc./Bridgeport, CT

ISBN 0-9615005-1-4

Library of Congress Catalog Card Number 85-81108

Design by Alice Cooke, A to Z Design

Cover Design by Alice Cooke; Illustration by Debby Dixler

Edited by Lisa Lyons Durkin

Associate Editor: Francesca DeMaria
Skills Chart by Martha A. Hayes

Manufactured in the United States of America

Published by First Teacher Press, First Teacher Inc.
P.O. Box 29, 60 Main Street, Bridgeport, CT 06602

THE TABLE OF CONTENTS

CONTENTS

WE BELIEVE THAT

■ children have the right to nutritionally good foods, prepared properly and attractively.

■ children have the right to learn about foods and their nutritional value in order to make good food choices.

■ children have the right to a better understanding of the role of food for good health so that they can develop sensible eating habits.

■ children have the right to be actively involved in preparing foods they will eat, as a way to promote independence and develop self confidence.

■ children can learn many skills and concepts from the preparation of foods.

■ children can learn a sense of community through the sharing of food preparation and eating.

CHILDREN AND COOKING

"Cooking is an exciting way to learn concepts and skills."

"The best recipes allow children the most participation."

"Classroom cooking has something to benefit everyone."

Cooking has it all. It offers an exciting way to learn all sorts of concepts from shapes to opposites. It is full of new vocabulary. It provides "real" work for young children, as they develop their small motor skills and their senses of touch, taste, and smell. It develops their abstract thinking skills with experiences in cause and effect, recall, and sequence. The rewards of cooking are so much more than the enjoyment of a delicious, final product.

Cooking with children is different from "cooking three meals a day," with which most of us are familiar. Before starting, you have to select the most appropriate recipe for the skills and concepts you wish to teach. Sometimes, it is better to choose a dough that can be kneaded and freeformed, rather than one that is mixed and dropped from a spoon. The best recipes are those which allow children the most participation. Children should be able to gather the ingredients, to "read" the recipe, to measure, mix, and serve. The whole process is important. This is when and where the real learning occurs. The final product is a bonus.

When we cook with children, we should always be aware of what they are learning. As adults, we often measure and mix automatically; yet, to the child, the very act of pouring water into a measuring cup to the correct level is Math, small motor coordination, and Science. (Remember, children must learn that liquids take the shape of the container.) If we recognize that all these things are taking place, we can guide our children's learning more fully.

Cooking with children can be more fun than cooking by ourselves. Children delight in feeling the textures of the ingredients. They offer opinions, often very humorous, about the tastes and smells of everything. They get into the whole process so intensely that it is a pleasure to watch.

Cooking as a classroom activity is highly motivating. It has something to benefit everyone. There are usually enough steps to provide individual jobs for even a large group. Many a "problem child" has settled down, while painstakingly chopping celery for soup. This is important work, just like Mom and Dad do at home. And, it is all topped off by the wonderful experience of sharing the food that was make by cooperative hands.

CONCEPTS AND COOKING

Cooking with children is amazingly adaptable. It fits right into most areas of the curriculum. In an Early Childhood classroom, cooking can be part of Science, Math, Social Studies, Language Development, and Fine Arts.

For example, cooking with apples can be integrated into each subject area.

"Cooking is Science."

Cooking is SCIENCE when a child picks up an apple and wonders how it got to be that size, and then, predicts what will happen to it as it is made into applesauce. Cooking helps children to:

■ understand the growth process — where foods come from, when they are available, and the various parts of plants we use as food.
■ understand how our bodies use food and the effects various food have on us.
■ understand how food is changed through the addition of heat or cold.
■ understand that single ingredients can be combined to make an entirely different product, such as eggs, flour, sugar, and milk, making a cake; yet, the cake can never again be broken down into its components.
■ understand better the principles of Science and experimentation. If mistakes are made, children can see how they happened and could have been avoided.

"Cooking is Math."

Cooking is MATH when a child looks at the apple, cuts it into six parts, calls each a "wedge," and cooks the pieces for 10 minutes to make applesauce. Cooking experiences help children to:

■ count money to buy ingredients.
■ decide on amounts of ingredients, practicing skills, such as measuring, weighing, counting, sorting, and estimating.
■ keep time with a clock or timer.
■ deal with parts of wholes or fractional parts, when proportioning out final results.
■ experience one-to-one correspondence, when cooking three pancakes for three children.
■ recognize shapes in various foods.
■ use graphs to chart food likes and dislikes.

"Cooking is Social Studies."

Cooking is SOCIAL STUDIES when a child learns that apples were shipped by truck from the Pacific Northwest to the local store, so that he could make apple strudel like his German grandma, and then, share it with the others in the class. Children's experiences in cooking help them to:

- learn how to work cooperatively on a cooking project.
- appreciate and value the role of family members in providing their food.
- learn to prepare foods from other countries, as well as foods from their own ethnic backgrounds.
- learn to share the final cooked meals or snacks with others.
- understand where and how foods are grown and transported to them for use.
- learn about their community, when purchasing foods.

"Cooking is Language Arts and Reading."

Cooking is LANGUAGE ARTS and READING when a child uses pictures to "read" the recipe for Blender Applesauce, and then, recalls the details and retells how he made the applesauce, step by step. Cooking helps children to:

- "read" recipes and books with picture aids.
- "write" illustrated recipes, grocery lists, and cooking stories.
- recall the sequence of recipe steps and recite them orally.
- use and understand new words, especially the action and description words of cooking.
- see words that represent actual ingredients.

"Cooking is Fine Arts."

Cooking is FINE ARTS when a child sings as he cuts red, green, and yellow apple slices and makes a flower with a peanut butter and raisin center. Cooking experiences help children to:

- use creativity in choosing and preparing foods.
- learn to appreciate and use various colors of foods.
- recreate the cooking experience in art media.
- "sing" as they work, in a traditional worksong manner.
- serve food in an attractive manner with decorative place settings.

HOW TO USE THIS BOOK

"In this book, cooking is integrated into all aspects of children's learning."

CONCEPT COOKERY is organized into conceptual and theme areas. Experience shows that most curriculum for young children is thematic. So, this book is divided into subjects, such as "Colors," "Holidays," "Seasons," "Numbers," and so on. This will enable you to fit the activities directly into your existing lesson plans. In this way, cooking is integrated into all aspects of children's learning. Read the suggested pre- and follow up activities for each recipe to help you decide how to fit it into your curriculum.

CONCEPT COOKERY is special in that each recipe is presented in such a way that the child can read along with you, following the sequential picture steps. Unless specifically designated as an adult activity (usually for safety reasons), children should be able to do or help you do each step.

"Children 'read' each recipe by following sequential picture steps."

Hang a copy of the recipe in the cooking center each week. There are enough for every week of the school year. Send a copy home for parents to do with their child. Add comments to inform parents of the concepts their child is learning by doing this particular activity. Use these same formats to make your own recipes. Use these recipes as is or change them to fit the needs of the children with whom you are working.

The charts on the next two pages tell you which thinking and pre-reading skills are highlighted in each recipe. Cooking can be a fun-filled way to help a child who is having particular difficulty with a skill. It is also a pressureless method parents can use to practice the skill with their child.

"Work with a few children or the whole group, using the assembly line or kit method."

Generally, it is easiest for one adult to work with small groups of three or four children at a time. In this manner, you can cook with the whole class on a rotating basis during the morning or afternoon. However, some of the recipes can be "put together," so that the whole class can work on them at one time. Recipes, such as Melon Boats, Animal Sandwiches, Humpty Egg, and the "Me" Salad can be done by everyone at once, using the assembly line technique. You set out the ingredients and the children make their choices and put the dish together. Another successful technique is the "kit method." You place the individual ingredients in ziplock bags, one for each child.

PRE-READING SKILLS HIGHLIGHTED IN COOKING PROJECTS

	Cause and Effect	Classification	Comparison	Details	Following Directions	Main Idea	Math	Motor Development	Opposites	Part to Whole	Relationships -Color	Relationships -Shapes	Predicting Outcomes	Sequence
A "Me" Salad (page 29)		X		X		X				X		X	X	X
Bread Faces (30)	X				X	X	X	X		X	X		X	X
All In a Cup Cooking (31)					X	X				X				
"I Can Do It Myself" Sandwiches (32)		X		X	X	X				X				
Blender Applesauce (35)			X		X	X	X			X				X
Nut Butters (36)		X	X	X	X			X	X				X	X
Jack O'Lantern Fruit Cup (37)		X			X	X				X		X		X
Turkey Soup (39)	X				X	X				X	X			X
Cranberry-Orange Relish (40)								X		X				
Birdseed Bread Wreath (41)	X			X	X			X		X	X		X	X
Fluffy Egg Nests (43)														
Open Animal Faced Sandwiches (44)		X	X	X		X		X		X			X	
Bird's Nest Salad (45)														
Ice Cream (47)	X		X		X				X			X		X
An At Home Camp Out (48)	X	X			X	X		X		X	X			X
Melon Boat (50)				X	X	X		X		X			X	
Jello-y Jewels (53)	X				X				X	X	X	X	X	X
Purple Cow Shakes (54)					X		X					X		X
Color-fool Foods (55)	X		X	X					X			X		
Rainbow Cookies (56)					X	X		X					X	X
Pretzels and Creative Twists (59)	X				X			X				X		X
Homemade Pasta (60)			X					X		X			X	X
Shortbread Puzzles (62)	X		X	X	X			X	X	X			X	X
Singing Salad (65)		X	X					X					X	

PRE-READING SKILLS HIGHLIGHTED IN COOKING PROJECTS

	Cause and Effect	Classification	Comparison	Details	Following Directions	Main Idea	Math	Motor Development	Opposites	Part to Whole	Relationships -Color	Relationships -Shapes	Predicting Outcomes	Sequence
Cottage Cheese (page 66)	X				X			X						
Snacks on a String (67)		X	X	X				X		X			X	
Sink and Float Jello (68)	X	X	X	X			X	X			X			
Jack Be Nimble (71)				X		X				X				
Play Foods (72)	X			X	X			X		X			X	
Humpty Dumpty Egg (74)				X				X		X			X	
"Grow It Again" (77)		X		X	X		X			X	X			
Butter (78)	X				X	X		X		X				
Yogurt (79)	X				X	X					X			
Jumping Raisins (80)	X		X		X				X					
Currant Buns (83)	X				X			X		X				
Big Batch of Gingerbread (84)	X			X	X	X		X		X			X	
The Perfect Pancake (85)				X	X	X				X				
Pumpkin Seeds (86)					X					X				
–Sicles (89)	X	X			X					X				
Cold Spaghetti Salad (90)					X	X		X		X				
Sweet/Sour Pickles (91)					X				X	X				
Maple Candy (92)							X	X	X	X				
Celebration Bread (96)	X	X		X	X	X		X			X		X	
Cake 'N Ice Cream (98)	X				X		X	X		X				X
Orange Sipper (99)	X				X			X			X			X
Apple from Outer Space (100)	X				X			X					X	X
Racers (101)		X		X	X	X		X		X			X	
Corn Doggies (102)	X			X	X	X		X		X				X
Pigs in Blankets (103)	X				X		X	X					X	
Fortune Cookies (104)					X				X	X	X		X	X

GETTING READY

As with any good teaching, preparation and organization are very important. When planning to cook with your class, you must consider:

■ the space you will be using;
■ the general equipment needed;
■ the ingredients needed;
■ safety and health rules;
■ how you and the children will participate in the process.

Here are some suggestions to get you started. Remember to make the most of what is readily available to you and adapt ideas to your own particular situation.

SETTING UP THE COOKING AREA

"You should have a cooking center and a dramatic play cooking area."

When setting up the cooking area, you must distinguish between the actual cooking center and the dramatic play cooking area. The first is an adult and child workspace and the second is a roleplaying space with a few cooking utensils for children to reenact the real cooking they've done. This second area will be used much more often than the first, so your real cooking center can be as simple as a portable cart, a section of the meal preparation kitchen in a daycare center, or an empty, child-sized table in a corner, where you haul out equipment, stored in nearby cabinets.

If you are using a table as your area, cover it with clear plastic, a flannel-backed plastic tablecloth, or even clean brown paper. The paper is usually more sanitary and makes cleaning up faster and easier. You might want to cover the floors with one of these materials or newspapers.

"Here is a list of important equipment."

You should consider buying a few essential pieces of equipment that can be stored in cabinets — away from small, curious hands. This equipment could include:

- a mixer
- a whisk
- a blender
- a hot plate (if you don't have a stove)
- an electric frying pan
- a timer
- a saucepan
- a deep pot
- a set of measuring spoons
- a set of measuring cups
- a one cup liquid measuring cup
- one or two cookie sheets
- a rubber spatula
- wooden spoons
- mixing bowls
- a grater
- knives (sharp metal ones for adult use, plastic ones for children)
- a colander
- a rolling pin
- a chopping board
- pot holders
- muffin tins
- a loaf pan

Don't forget to ask parents for contributions before you head for the store. Even a pot with a hole in the bottom can be used in the dramatic play area. Childmade cookie sales during the year can help pay for the items you must buy.

"Keep a cabinet of food staples."

Keep a cabinet stocked with food staples, such as flour, salt, macaroni, yeast, baking powder and soda, dry milk powder, gelatin, evaporated milk, and spices. It is best to keep these items in tins or tightly sealed containers to avoid attracting bugs or rodents. Most of the other ingredients can be brought in, when needed.

"Make a box where parents can drop off ingredients."

Or, you can put out a call to parents for special ingredients. Use the convenient letter on the next page. Make a copy, fill in the ingredients you'll need, and send home. A "Little Cook's Box" should be located in the arrival area, so it will remind parents of your request, as well as be a convenient place to drop off the ingredients on the cooking day.

WHAT'S COOKING?

Dear _____ ,

   We will be cooking on _____ (date) and would be grateful if you could help us by providing part of the ingredients. We will be making _____ (food) and need _____ (amount and name of ingredient). Please drop it off to us on or before the above date.

   Thank you for your continuing cooperation.

_____
Your Child's Teacher

JOB CHART

Part of the whole cooking experience is social. Each child should feel essential to the functioning of the group. Each child should feel respect for others' tasks and courtesy toward each participant.

A job chart can help make the cooking experience more manageable as well as enjoyable for all. Use this design. Make a large one from posterboard. Write in the jobs suggested or any of your own. With tape, attach a name tag to each job. Rotate jobs for each cooking experience.

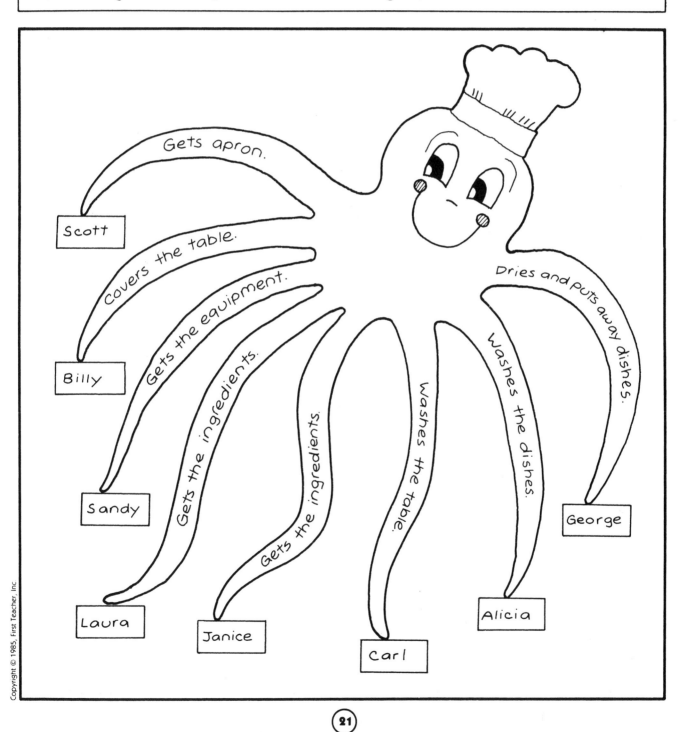

SAFETY AND HEALTH

"Electrical appliances and stoves should be used only by adults."

1. Demonstrate and let children practice using utensils. These can include a whisk, measuring spoons and cups, a spatula, strainer or colander, wooden spoons, and rolling pin. Under close supervision, some children can use a vegetable peeler and a grater.
2. Store all utensils out of children's reach.
3. Electrical appliances, such as mixers, blenders, frying pans, or hot plates, should be used by ADULTS ONLY.
4. Young children should not use the stove at all.
5. When using small appliances around children, set them next to you with cords well out of the way of children.

HEALTH RULES

"Food should always be fresh and of good quality."

1. Check every child's record for any food allergy. If someone gets an allergic reaction, stay away from the preparation of that particular food, so the child will not be tempted and/or feel left out, when he is unable to join the cooking/eating experience.
2. Make sure all utensils are perfectly clean and sanitary, before using.
3. Make sure all hands are absolutely clean before cooking.
4. Children with obvious colds or diseases that are catching should not participate in any cooking experience, while they are infected.
5. Food should be fresh and of good quality. If refrigeration is required, use it promptly. IF IN DOUBT, THROW IT OUT.
6. Make sure hot foods are thoroughly cooked and any leftovers are quickly refrigerated.
7. Instruct children in advance how to deal with a sneeze or a cough. (Cover mouth and turn away; then, wash hands immediately.)
8. Children should not put food into their mouths while cooking, unless instructed otherwise.

APRONS

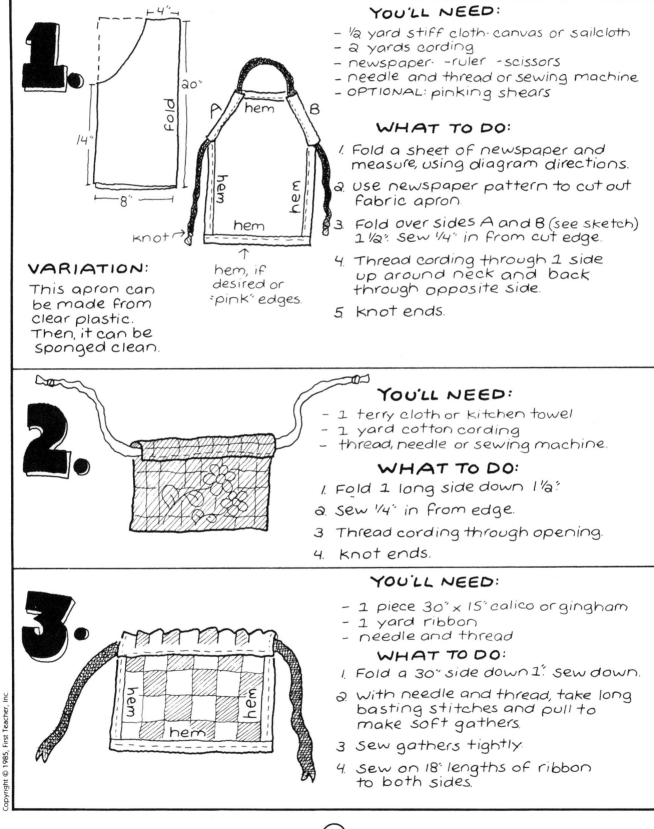

1.

YOU'LL NEED:

- ½ yard stiff cloth· canvas or sailcloth
- 2 yards cording
- newspaper· -ruler -scissors
- needle and thread or sewing machine
- OPTIONAL: pinking shears

WHAT TO DO:

1. Fold a sheet of newspaper and measure, using diagram directions.
2. Use newspaper pattern to cut out fabric apron.
3. Fold over sides A and B (see sketch) 1½". Sew ¼" in from cut edge.
4. Thread cording through 1 side up around neck and back through opposite side.
5. Knot ends.

4"
20"
14"
8"
Fold
hem
A
B
hem
hem
hem
knot →
hem, if desired or "pink" edges.

VARIATION:

This apron can be made from clear plastic. Then, it can be sponged clean.

2.

YOU'LL NEED:

- 1 terry cloth or kitchen towel
- 1 yard cotton cording
- thread, needle or sewing machine.

WHAT TO DO:

1. Fold 1 long side down 1½".
2. Sew ¼" in from edge.
3. Thread cording through opening.
4. Knot ends.

3.

YOU'LL NEED:

- 1 piece 30" x 15" calico or gingham
- 1 yard ribbon
- needle and thread

WHAT TO DO:

1. Fold a 30" side down 1". sew down.
2. With needle and thread, take long basting stitches and pull to make soft gathers.
3. Sew gathers tightly.
4. Sew on 18" lengths of ribbon to both sides.

hem
hem
hem

AT THE SUPERMARKET

"You can develop skills and concepts at the supermarket."

Start your cooking experiences at the supermarket or the corner grocery store. Hidden among those boxes, cans, containers, on the shelves, over ice, and in glass cases, are some of the best lessons that you can find in Math, Language Development, Science, and Social Studies.

Before you even get to the market, do a few things to help make the trip more meaningful for the young shopper.

1. Make a shopping list with the children. First, read the recipe together. Then, write and illustrate each ingredient. The list can be broken up so each child has one item to look for.

2. Determine how much you will need to purchase and approximately how much money you will need to spend. Count out that approximate amount beforehand with the children.

"Make a 'Let's See' list."

3. Discuss what you will probably see at the market. Make a *"Let's See"* list of things to notice.

   ■ Look for unusual fruits and vegetables in the produce department. (Does anyone know their names?)

   ■ Look for live fish and lobsters in tanks. (Why do they keep them in water?)

   ■ Look for scales in the produce department. Weigh something. Guess which of two things weighs the most.

   ■ Look at the freezers. (Do they have doors? How do things stay cold?)

   ■ Look for a bakery. (Can you tell if the store has one without seeing it?)

   ■ Look for machines that make juice, grind coffee, or slice meat. Watch how they work.

   ■ Look at the checkout counters. (Do they have talking computers?)

4. Discuss supermarket manners, behavior, and safety, with the children.

"Take only a small group each trip."

Take only a small, easily managed group to the market at one time. Go down each aisle to notice the items on your *"Let's See"* list, as well as to give the children the opportunity to find grocery list items. Point out where the items can be found. For example, milk can be found in the refrigerated section.

The supermarket is the perfect place to raise *"Where does it come from?"* questions. Have children notice the various vegetables. Point out the ones, like potatoes, carrots, beets, and radishes, that grow underground. Compare them to vegetables that grow above ground.

"Point out signs in the market."

Remember Language Arts by pointing out a few signs. See if the children can read the SALE signs, that are placed in many locations around the store. The children will notice that many cans and packages are illustrated with food items. Back in the classroom, you might want to use can and box labels to make a "Match" shopping list. Mount the labels and descriptive pictures on cards and use them as your list, the next time you shop.

Show children different forms of the same food. Corn can be found fresh on the cob, in cans, in bags of cornmeal, as cornmeal muffins in the bakery section, and even in bags as corn chips!

Look at the colors of the packaging. Point out the fact that each company has its own special colors and/or symbol. Ask children what colors they see most often on packages.

When all the items have been gathered, check out. Observe how the bags are packed. Let the children tell you why the heavy items are on the bottom and the light ones are on the top.

"Play learning games back in the classroom."

After the supermarket and cooking experience, have children play some or all of these games.

■ Make play foods to use in the dramatic play area. See directions on page 72.

■ Make a map of the supermarket. Illustrate the large, general sections. Then, have children pick cards with food items drawn or pasted on from labels. They must put the food in the correct section on the map. For example, the card with ice cream on it goes in the dairy section. A picture of corn on the cob goes in the produce department.

■ Clean and save all empty containers and set up a supermarket in the classroom. Have brown bags, play money, and a cash register.

■ Save empty containers and set out brown bags with a letter of the alphabet written on each one. Have the children put the can for peas and the bag for peanuts in the bag marked with a "P."

■ Let children sort the empty containers according to categories, such as "fruits," "vegetables," "dairy," "meats," and "pasta." Include different forms of containers, like cans and boxes, and play foods.

"Teach children where foods come from."

■ With the children, make charts of "Where Did It Come From?" Then, make a poster divided into three parts: the ocean, the land, and a grouping of animals, including chickens, pigs, cows, and sheep. Make up cards with familiar foods. Include bacon, eggs, fish, clams, milk, cheese, bananas. . . Let children sort the cards according to where they come from.

ALL ABOUT ME

ALL ABOUT ME

This is a popular theme in classes of young children, especially at the beginning of the year. In keeping with the goals of this unit, cooking experiences give each child the sense that he can do important work by himself, and, at the same time, make a contribution to a group activity. Use these cooking projects to get to know each child better and to observe each learning style.

"Me" Salad

The "Me" Salad is an old-fashioned fun lunch, popular since Grandma's time. It offers good, nutritious foods with definite "I" appeal. Again, you set the limits by putting out the ingredients and offering suggestions on how to assemble the salad. You might make charts with the children to show how "Me" Salads might look, as long as this doesn't discourage creativity.

Bread Faces

Bread Faces are fun and relatively inexpensive to make, using materials generally found on your staples shelf. This recipe allows for maximum participation by your children. Mixing and handling doughs give them the opportunity to use their tactile sense, as well as their senses of taste, sight, and smell. And, the more senses a child uses, the better the learning will be. Use this recipe to observe how each child works. Some will take time pinching and adding bits of dough. Others will make a few additions and be done. These insights will help you guide the child in other areas, as well.

All in a Cup Cooking

These recipes help children become more independent. You set out the ingredients and you determine the serving amount by using the five ounce cup. But, the child gets the opportunity to add his own creative touches and then, eat his creation in an individual container.

The paper cup can be used for other cooking experiences, also. Fill an unwaxed paper hot cup half way with muffin batter. Bake in a 350 degree oven for 15 - 20 minutes. Cool and let children scoop on some frozen yogurt or cooked berries. They will love their own serving of this delicious treat.

"I Can Do It Myself" Sandwiches

"I can do it myself" is a familiar phrase around young children, especially two and three year olds. Use this recipe to satisfy their need for independence. Most children will probably use the freedom in this recipe to make wise food choices and combinations. Yet, sometimes, a child will make weird combinations or build ridiculous creations. Don't make the child eat it if he doesn't want to. Remove him from the situation and talk about what he should be doing. Give him a chance to try it again in the correct way.

A ME SALAD

YOU'LL NEED:
- cottage cheese
- ½ hard-boiled egg - 1 per child
- carrot and celery sticks
- alfalfa sprouts
- lettuce leaves
- shredded cheese
- pimento slices
- spoons
- bowls
- ½ canned peach - 1 per child
- paper plates

WHAT TO DO:

1. Set out ingredients buffet style.

2. Talk about what kind of person each child would like to make.

3. Choose the foods needed to make the people for the "me salads."

½ hard-boiled egg

alfalfa sprouts

pimento

carrot stick

shredded cheese

raisin

pimento

cottage cheese

½ canned peach

celery stick

carrot stick

½ canned peach underneath lettuce leaf

BREAD FACES

YOU'LL NEED:

FLOUR — 2 cups flour — 3/4 cup ice cold water — OIL — 3 Tblsp. oil — 1/2 tsp. salt — bowl — polyurethane — paintbrush — 4 8" aluminum pie plates — cookie sheets — metal table knife (ADULT USE ONLY)

WHAT TO DO:

1. Measure flour and salt in a bowl.

2. Add oil and rub it in until mixture resembles coarse oatmeal.

3. Add 3/4 cup water. Blend with fingers. Add more water, if needed, to form a dough. Gather into a ball.

4. Knead 10 minutes.

5. Divide dough into 4-6 balls. Roll each 8" in diameter.

6. Place on the flat bottom of an inverted pie plate

dough

inverted pie plate

7. Adult cuts in features with a knife. Pinch features in dough with fingers and attach other features with pieces of dough. Attach dough to dough with water.

8. Place pie plates on cookie sheets. Bake in 350°F oven for 10-15 minutes.

cut out, pinch, and add on features

9. Eat or display.

TO DISPLAY:

Place "faces" in 250°F oven for 6-8 hours. Cool. Cover with polyurethane.

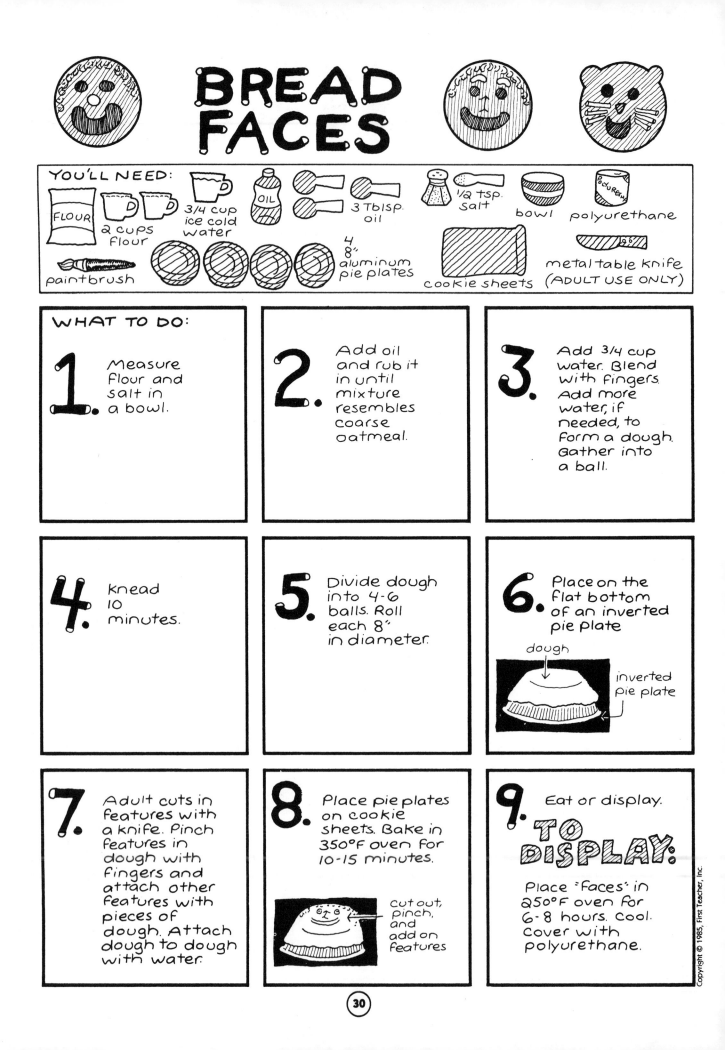

ALL IN ONE CUP COOKING

YOGURT PARFAIT

YOU'LL NEED:

plain yogurt- 1 large container

5 oz. paper cups

spoon

SOME OF THE FOLLOWING:

blueberries   raisins   nuts

banana slices   peach slices

shredded coconut   sunflower seeds

WHAT TO DO:

1. Set out the ingredients.

2. Create a parfait by layering yogurt, fruit, raisins... in a 5 oz. paper cup.

SIPPY DIPPERS

YOU'LL NEED:

sour cream

cottage cheese- it can be whipped smooth in a blender

5 oz. paper cups

SOME OF THE FOLLOWING:
- dill weed
- parsley
- celery seed
- paprika

-Herbs and spices-

chopped green onions

fresh vegetables

WHAT TO DO:

1. Set out ingredients. Talk about making a dip. Explain that the largest amount in a dip is the sour cream and cottage cheese. Caution that each herb is strong and only a small bit is needed.

2. Make and flavor dips in 5 oz. cups.

3. Eat with fresh, raw vegetables.

FRUIT SODA

YOU'LL NEED:

club soda   orange juice   grape juice

cranberry juice   apple juice   5 oz. paper cups

WHAT TO DO:

1. Set out the ingredients.

2. Pour fruit juice into cup and add club soda.

3. Make 1 flavor or combine for fruit punch.

FRUIT SODA

31

I CAN DO IT MYSELF SANDWICHES

YOU'LL NEED: -Washed and sliced vegetables and fruits-

cucumber   tomato   banana   apple   pear   carrot   zucchini

-Fillings-

PEANUT BUTTER peanut butter   whipped cream cheese   American cheese slices   MAYO mayonnaise   plastic knife

WHAT TO DO

1. Place a few sliced fruits or vegetables in small dishes.

2. Place 1 or 2 fillings in a dish.

3. Make sandwiches such as:

vegetable or fruit
↓
←filling
vegetable or fruit

SANDWICH SNACKS

outsides	Insides

PEANUT BUTTER

MAYO

Make a chart.

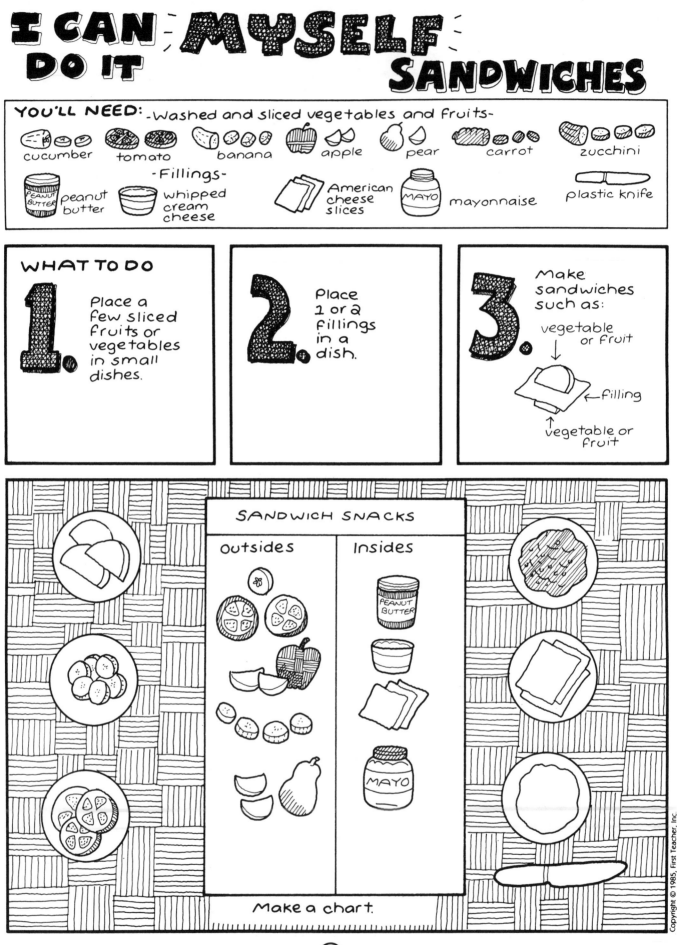

THE SEASONS

Very often, ideas for recipes are dictated by the seasons. Traditionally, cooks have used foods ''in season'' when they are readily available and the freshest. Also, we make certain foods because they are associated with holidays or the lifestyles of the seasons.

The following recipes draw on both of these concepts. Don't hesitate to fit them into other areas and themes you are developing. For example, Melon Boats could fit into a unit on transportation and Bird's Nest Salad could be used when you are discussing the habits of animals. Also, if you find one recipe is a particular favorite of your children, use it several times during the year.

FALL

The word *"fall"* brings to mind apples for the teacher, piles of leaves, falling acorns, and a full harvest moon over fields of pumpkins. Even if this is just a picturebook autumn in your part of the country, fall does signify a transition. And, with it, comes the harvest and holiday foods.

Blender Applesauce

Most children are getting back to school and this is a wonderfully easy recipe to start off the year. They can even participate in the cutting, using plastic knives. Apples can be used for many easy recipes, including the following.

■ Make applesauce, without peeling the apples. Strain through a colander or food mill. You will have Rosy Applesauce.

■ Peel the apples, cook until mushy, add a pinch of cinnamon, and spread very thinly on a pottery dish. Place in direct sunlight for a day or two. Peel the fruit leather off the plate for a special snack.

■ Peel apples, cut into ⅛ inch slices, and string on a thread with a needle. Hang in a warm, dry place. After a few days, the apples will dry. Store in a closed jar.

Nut Butters

This cooking activity demonstrates how a favorite food of all children, peanut butter, is made. Children will love cracking the shells on various nuts. You might want to make a chart showing which nuts are hard to crack and which ones are easy.

Have a taste test of the different flavors of the nuts. Try them with toppings, such as bacon or banana, or with lettuce. Put a nut butter into celery, add raisins, and call it *"ants on a log."* Make a spread with a nut butter, grated carrot, and raisins.

Don't let children under four eat whole nuts. They are a prime cause of choking in very young children.

Jack O'Lantern Fruit Cup

This fruit salad is a wholesome alternative to sweeter Halloween treats. It provides children with lots of practice in scooping out and cutting up. And, it looks terrific!

This might be a good time to discuss the many fruits and vegetables that are orange in color. You can include pumpkins, winter squash, carrots, sweet potatoes, tangerines, cantaloupe, and oranges. These orange fruits and vegetables provide the vitamins A and C, which are important for good skin and eyes, healthy bones and teeth.

BLENDER APPLESAUCE

YOU'LL NEED:

6 apples · ½ cup honey · few drops of water · peeler · plastic knife · blender

WHAT TO DO:

1. Peel the apples.

2. Cut each apple into 4 pieces.

3. Put apples, honey, and a small amount of water into the blender.

4. Blend until smooth. Enjoy!

YUM!

Copyright © 1985, First Teacher, Inc.

NUT BUTTERS (AND OTHER NUT IDEAS)

YOU'LL NEED:

1 cup nuts

blender

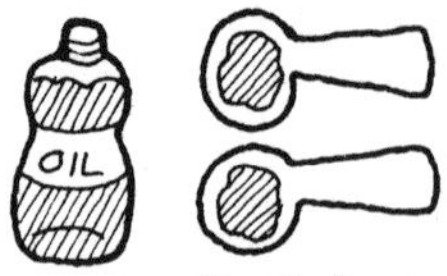

2 Tblsp salad oil

OPTIONAL: pinch of salt and/or sugar

WHAT TO DO:

1. ☆ Here is a list of nuts most commonly found in supermarkets:

- almond
- Brazil
- cashew
- chestnut

- filbert
- macadamia
- peanut

- pine
- pistachio
- walnut

2. ☆ Talk about the color, shape, texture, and hardness of the nut shells. Try various ways of cracking the shells.....

with your hands.

against each other.

with a rock.

with a hammer.

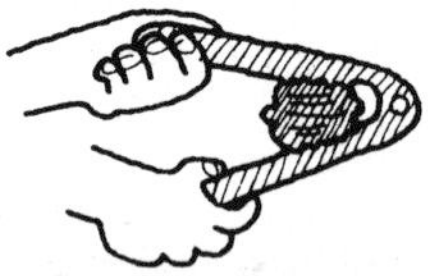

with a nut cracker

3. TO MAKE **NUT BUTTERS**

1. Place 1 cup nuts in blender jar.

2. Add 1-2 Tblsp. salad oil. Blend until smooth or crunchy. Taste.

3. Add a pinch of salt and/or a pinch of sugar, if desired.

JACK-O-LANTERN
FRUIT CUP

YOU'LL NEED:

orange

fruits

toothpick

felt tip marker

spoon

bowl

plastic knife (for children to use)

metal knife (ADULT USE ONLY)

WHAT TO DO:

1. Adult cuts off top of orange.

2. Scoop out insides and put into bowl.

3. Using a plastic knife, cut fruits.

4. Fill scooped-out orange with fruits.

scooped out orange

bowl of cut fruit

5. Replace top of orange. Stick together with a toothpick.

6. Draw on a face with a marker.

Copyright © 1985, First Teacher, Inc.

37

WINTER

Winter usually means lots of time indoors with holidays, hot cocoa, and friends, while outside, it is cold and damp. Warm everyone up with these winter recipes.

Turkey Soup

This recipe is a great way to use leftover turkey bones and meat. Children may enjoy adding more ingredients, such as beans, lentils, macaroni, and barley. They get very serious when chopping up vegetables with their plastic knives.

Hot soup can be dangerous around young children. Serve it slightly cooler than you would like it. If it is too hot, add an ice cube or two to each bowl to cool it down.

Cranberry Orange Relish

This recipe makes a lovely gift to send home to parents during the holidays. It can be refrigerated for two weeks. The jar can be decorated with a figure, using a construction paper head and cotton ball hair and beard.

Use the experience to talk about the cranberry. If possible, get pictures that show how the cranberry grows in bogs; how the bogs are often flooded to protect them from heat, cold, and insects; and how the berries are harvested with special rakes. Cook some cranberries to make jellied sauce. (The recipe is on the package.) Children enjoy watching and hearing the cranberries "pop," as they cook. Read the book, *Cranberry Thanksgiving*, and try the recipe for cranberry bread.

Birdseed Bread Wreath

Working with doughs is a satisfying cooking experience for most children. Accept whatever shape they construct. It is the manipulation they love. If the bread comes out in a circle, hang it on an outside door for the birds. If it turns out to be a blob, just use it for great eating.

While working with this recipe, mention to the children that food gives us energy. Birds get energy from food, also. A small bird may eat ⅓ of its weight each day to keep warm and full of energy. You may choose to make some other food for the birds during the winter. Hang outside pinecones stuffed with melted suet or bacon grease, mixed with peanut butter and rolled in birdseed. Fill empty orange or grapefruit cups with birdseed, and hang with string on trees. Use a needle and thread to string bits of suet, orange sections, cranberries, popcorn, and even chunks of doughnuts, and hang it all over a bush or a tree.

TURKEY SOUP

YOU'LL NEED:

turkey bones with a little meat on them — large pot — ½ cup peas — ½ cup diced carrot — ½ cup cooked rice — parsley — salt and pepper-to taste — spoon — serrated plastic knife — 1 onion-chopped — 2 potatoes-diced — 2 or 3 celery stalks-diced — OPTIONAL- 3 cans of chicken broth — vegetable peeler

WHAT TO DO:

1. Fill a large kettle 2/3 full with water or chicken broth. Adult places on stove and brings to a boil.

2. Add turkey bones. Simmer 1 hour. Adult removes carcass and loose bones. Leave broth in pot.

3. Add chopped onion, diced celery, peas, diced carrot, rice, diced potatoes. parsley. Simmer for 30 minutes. Add salt and pepper to taste.

CRANBERRY-ORANGE RELISH

YOU'LL NEED:

food chopper

2 large oranges

4 cups cranberries

sugar-to-taste

empty, clean baby food jars

glue

tape

scissors

crayons or markers

assorted decorating materials - for jars

WHAT TO DO:

construction paper rolled into tube and taped - for head

draw on a face

baby food jar filled with relish

cotton ball

ribbon

paper or fabric scrap mittens

cotton ball or fabric beard

SAMPLE CRANBERRY-ORANGE RELISH JAR

1. Divide oranges into 1/8's. Remove seeds.

2. Put orange sections and cranberries through the coarse blade of a food chopper. Add sugar- to taste.

3. Store in clean, empty baby food jars. Decorate.

40

BIRD SEED WREATH

YOU'LL NEED:

FLOUR — 4-4½ cups flour

2 Tblsp. sugar

1 tsp. salt

2 pkgs. yeast

1 cup milk

½ cup water

4 Tblsp. margarine

bowls

saucepan

sesame seeds

hulled sunflower seeds

2 egg WHITES

egg beater

waxed paper

pastry brush

ribbon

WHAT TO DO:

1. In a bowl, place sugar, yeast, and 2 cups of flour.

2. In a saucepan, heat until very warm (120°F) milk, water, and margarine.

3. Add warm liquid to dry ingredients and beat well by hand or with mixer.

4. Add rest of flour. Mix well. knead about 5 minutes.

5. Place in a greased bowl. Cover with a piece of greased waxed paper. Place in a very warm place (85°-90°F) for 15 minutes.

6. Take 2 good-sized balls of dough. Adult may show children how to roll into 12" long snakes. Twist the 2 long pieces together and form a circle. Seal ends with a little water and pinch. (older children might be able to braid 3 long pieces.)

7. Slightly beat egg whites with 1 tsp. water. Brush over tops of bread wreaths. Sprinkle seeds heavily over egg.

8. Place on a greased baking sheet. Allow to rise 15 minutes in a warm place.

9. Bake at 425°F for 12 minutes.

10. Cool. Tie a large bow on wreath. This wreath can be hung on an outside door for the birds to peck off the seeds. It also is good for people to eat.

SPRING

The egg, rebirth, and new life have come to symbolize the spirit of spring. In the Early Childhood classroom, spring is the time when pets are studied, hamster and guinea pig babies are born, and everyone goes on fieldtrips to the zoo. Thus, we have chosen recipes that use eggs or lead to discussions about animals.

Fluffy Egg Nests

Children are amazed by the egg. It can do so many different things. Here are some cooking experiments, using eggs.
- Crack open a raw egg. Show the yolk, white, and the shell with the membrane. Make an eggnog with milk, sugar, and nutmeg.
- Gently, swirl a raw egg into boiling water to make a poached egg. Let children observe how the white appears from the clear part.
- Scramble an egg and cook with a little butter in a pan.
- Scramble an egg and stir into boiling chicken broth for delicious egg drop soup.

Open Animal Faced Sandwiches

These are the cutest looking, most taste tempting lunches, we know of. Children love to make them and eat them. They make festive dishes for any party, especially one with an animal theme. They also help children develop the skill of looking for details because each animal has a different head with different parts and coloring.

Bird's Nest Salad

You cannot help but observe the activities of birds in the spring. You may see them flying overhead with string in their beaks or you may discover broken shells under a tree. If you're very lucky, you might even come across eggs in a nest and be able to observe them hatching.

Use this recipe in conjunction with a discussion about birds in the spring. Children will enjoy putting it together and talking about what a real bird might do to make a nest.

After you boil the egg in the shell, have children guess what it will look like when you open it. Some children have never seen a hardboiled egg before.

FLUFFY EGG NESTS

YOU'LL NEED:

- ◯◯ 2 eggs
- 2 pieces hot buttered toast
- salt   pepper
- bowl
- rotary beater -or-

WHAT TO DO:

1. Separate eggs. Put whites in a bowl. Leave yolks in the shell.

2. Beat egg white with a rotary beater or mixer until stiff enough to form peaks.

3. Heap onto toast. Make a hollow in the center of both mounds.

4. Slip egg yolks into hollow. Sprinkle with salt and pepper.

5. Bake at 350°F until meringue whites are browned and yolk is as you like it.

egg white meringue

egg yolk

toast

OPEN ANIMAL FACED SANDWICHES

YOU'LL NEED:

BREAD SLICES — white, whole wheat, pumpernickel — 4" cookie cutter -or- drinking glass with 3" opening

FILLINGS such as — luncheon meats, cheese slices, cream cheese, cottage cheese

TRIMS such as — raisins, olives, pimento, cherries, celery, carrots

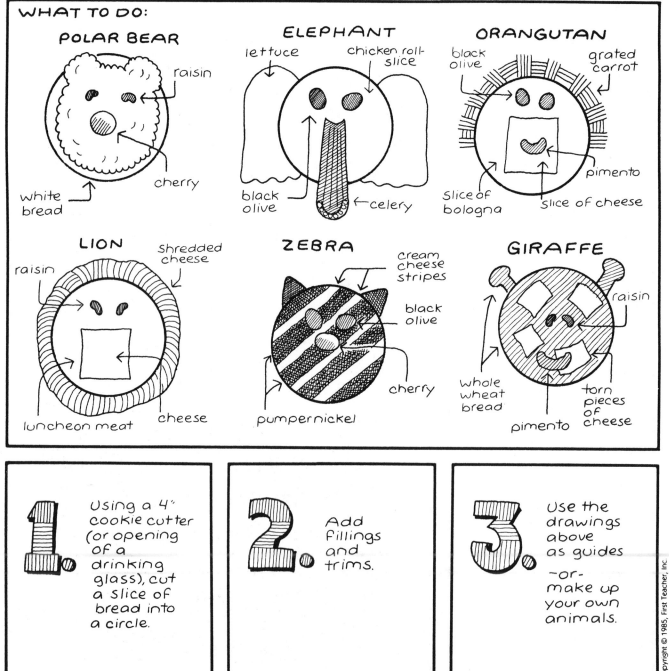

WHAT TO DO:

POLAR BEAR — raisin, cherry, white bread

ELEPHANT — lettuce, chicken roll-slice, black olive, celery

ORANGUTAN — black olive, grated carrot, pimento, Slice of bologna, slice of cheese

LION — raisin, shredded cheese, luncheon meat, cheese

ZEBRA — cream cheese stripes, black olive, cherry, pumpernickel

GIRAFFE — raisin, whole wheat bread, pimento, torn pieces of cheese

1. Using a 4" cookie cutter (or opening of a drinking glass), cut a slice of bread into a circle.

2. Add fillings and trims.

3. Use the drawings above as guides -or- make up your own animals.

BIRD'S NEST EGG SALAD

YOU'LL NEED:

plastic strawberry boxes

radishes, celery sticks, carrot sticks

hard-boiled eggs

lettuce OR chicory

plastic knife

WHAT TO DO:

1. Line strawberry box with lettuce OR chicory.

2. Fill with chopped egg salad or sliced egg.

3. Add assorted fresh vegetables.

sliced hard-boiled egg

radish

celery sticks

lettuce OR chicory

strawberry box "bird's nest"

SUMMER

Summertime has its own set of cooking and eating rules. Almost everywhere, there is heat and humidity and cooking usually takes a back seat to the put together meal or snack. Fast and refreshing are the words to describe summer recipes.

Ice Cream

Always a treat, ice cream can be a bother to make. This recipe has two pluses. It does not require a commercial ice cream maker, rock salt, and cracked ice, and it does not use raw eggs, which can be unhealthy, if not totally fresh and pure. Discuss the changes the ingredients go through from the whipping to the freezing. Let the children describe the taste of the ice cream and compare it to other ice cream they've had. Make a graph and let children see the favorite flavor ice creams of all the children.

To extend this activity, make lemon sherbet and have children compare its taste and texture to homemade ice cream. For the sherbet, you'll need: 1 lemon, juice and rind; 1 cup of sugar; 2 cups of milk. First, place sugar, lemon juice, and rind in a pan. Stir well. Slowly, add milk and mix until the sugar dissolves. Freeze until partially frozen. Then, break up the crystals with a fork. Freeze again until firm, and enjoy.

An At Home Camp Out

You needn't go to the Grand Canyon or even to the nearest campgrounds to use these camp-out recipes. They give children the flavor of a camp out just by the unique approach to preparing and cooking the foods.

The important thing to remember is that camp-out cooking is slower than stove cooking and must be carefully supervised and constantly watched by an adult. Children can help prepare the foods and watch them cooking. In the meanwhile, they can prepare cool accompaniments. Have them make "walking salads" (a small apple, filled with a mixture of peanut butter and raisins), or "wrap ups" (bologna and lettuce, wrapped around a cheese stick), or "mini-kabobs" (thin carrot sticks speared through cubes of cheese, luncheon meats, pickles, and olives).

Melon Boat

This recipe is a child pleaser! Children love to put it together and enjoy eating the variety of tastes and textures. For a group of children, assemble the ingredients in a zip locking bag like a kit; then pass them out to children for construction.

This recipe has a festive flair to it and is great for parties.

ICE CREAM

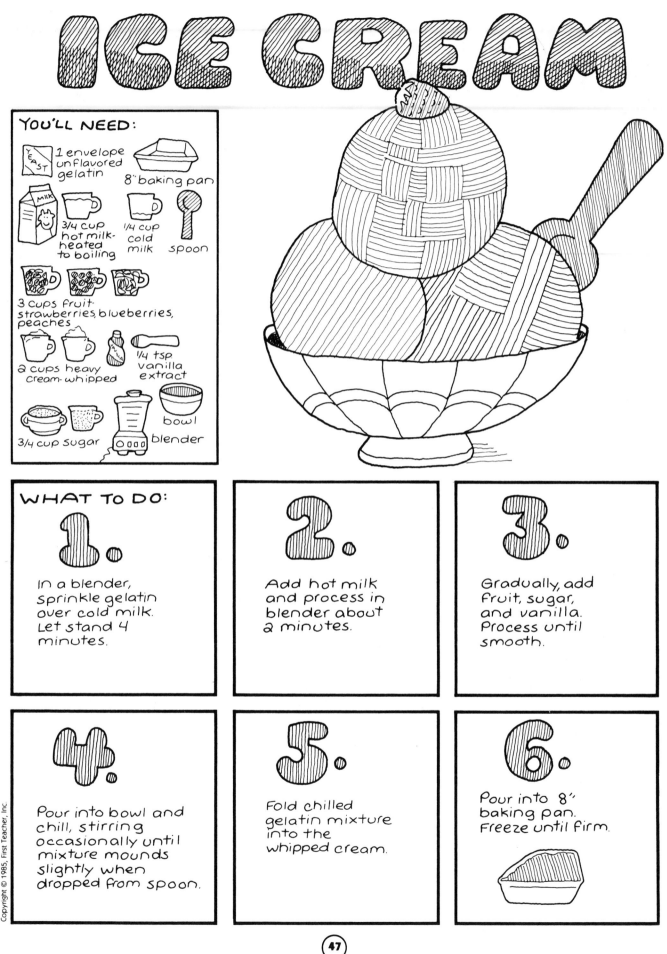

YOU'LL NEED:

1 envelope unflavored gelatin

8" baking pan

3/4 cup hot milk - heated to boiling

1/4 cup cold milk

spoon

3 cups fruit - strawberries, blueberries, peaches

2 cups heavy cream - whipped

1/4 tsp. vanilla extract

3/4 cup sugar

bowl

blender

WHAT TO DO:

1. In a blender, sprinkle gelatin over cold milk. Let stand 4 minutes.

2. Add hot milk and process in blender about 2 minutes.

3. Gradually, add fruit, sugar, and vanilla. Process until smooth.

4. Pour into bowl and chill, stirring occasionally until mixture mounds slightly when dropped from spoon.

5. Fold chilled gelatin mixture into the whipped cream.

6. Pour into 8" baking pan. Freeze until firm.

AN AT HOME CAMP OUT

PAN PIZZA

YOU'LL NEED:

- Frozen bread dough or hot roll mix
- 2 Tblsp. oil
- shredded mozzarella cheese or muenster cheese
- tomato sauce
- covered skillet
- spatula

WHAT TO DO:

1. Spread oil in skillet bottom.
2. Spread dough over entire bottom.
3. Cover tightly and cook slowly over coals about 6-8 minutes.
4. Turn over dough with a spatula.
5. Add sauce over dough.
6. Sprinkle with cheese.
7. Cover and continue baking until crust is baked and cheese is melted.

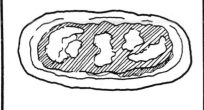

TWIG TOAST

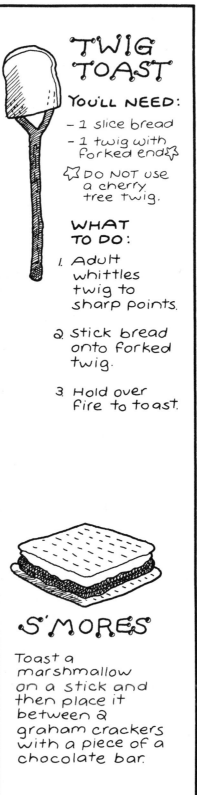

YOU'LL NEED:

- 1 slice bread
- 1 twig with forked end ☆
- ☆ DO NOT use a cherry tree twig.

WHAT TO DO:

1. Adult whittles twig to sharp points.
2. Stick bread onto forked twig.
3. Hold over fire to toast.

S'MORES

Toast a marshmallow on a stick and then place it between 2 graham crackers with a piece of a chocolate bar.

CORN-ON-THE-COB

YOU'LL NEED:

- 1 ear of corn
- 1 Tblsp. butter
- 1 ice cube or 2 Tblsp. water
- aluminum foil

WHAT TO DO:

1. Put 1 ear of corn on a piece of aluminum foil.
2. Add 1 Tblsp. butter and 1 ice cube (or 2 Tblsp. water).
3. Wrap up foil. Secure tightly and twist ends.
4. Roast in coals or on a grill 10-15 minutes. Turn frequently.

butter

aluminum foil

ice cube

corn-on-the-cob

BAKED FRUIT DESSERTS

YOU'LL NEED:

- 1 apple
- 1 banana
- 2 Tblsp. mini-marshmallows
- 2 Tblsp. chocolate chips
- dash of cinnamon or whole cinnamon stick
- aluminum foil
- plastic knife
- apple corer

cinnamon stick

aluminum foil

WHAT TO DO:

1. Core apple. Sprinkle on cinnamon or force cinnamon stick through apple. Wrap in foil.

2. Cut a wedge of banana open, leaving peel intact. Stuff with mini-marshmallows and chocolate chips. Cover with cut peel. Wrap in foil.

3. Place near coals or on a grill. Cook banana until stuffing is melted. Cook apple until soft.

BOIL-IN-A-BAG CUSTARD

YOU'LL NEED:

- 1 egg, well-beaten with fork
- 3/4 cup milk
- 2 tsp. sugar
- dash of vanilla
- dash of cinnamon
- ziplocking bag
- deep pan of boiling water

WHAT TO DO:

1. Put all ingredients into zip locking bag. "Zip" closed.

2. Adult places bag in deep pan of boiling water.

3. Cook 6-10 minutes.

4. Adult removes bag from water.

5. Eat custard from bag or pour immediately into a bowl.

CINNAMON

VANILLA

DUMP SHORTCAKE

YOU'LL NEED:

- 1 lb. can of fruit cocktail or chunky fruits
- 2 cups biscuit mix
- 1/3 cup dry milk
- 1/4 cup sugar
- 1/3 cup water
- 1 egg, well-beaten with fork
- ziplocking bag
- covered skillet
- spatula
- OPTIONAL: cream

WHAT TO DO:

1. Dump can of fruit cocktail or chunky fruits into a heavy metal skillet.

2. Mix biscuit mix, dry milk, and sugar (these could be pre-mixed) in a ziplocking bag.

3. Add egg and water. Mix well.

4. Open 1 corner of bag and squeeze batter over fruit cocktail.

batter

fruit

5. Cover skillet tightly. Cook slowly over fire 30-40 minutes.

6. Remove cover. Flip shortcake onto plate. Serve with cream, if desired.

MELON BOAT

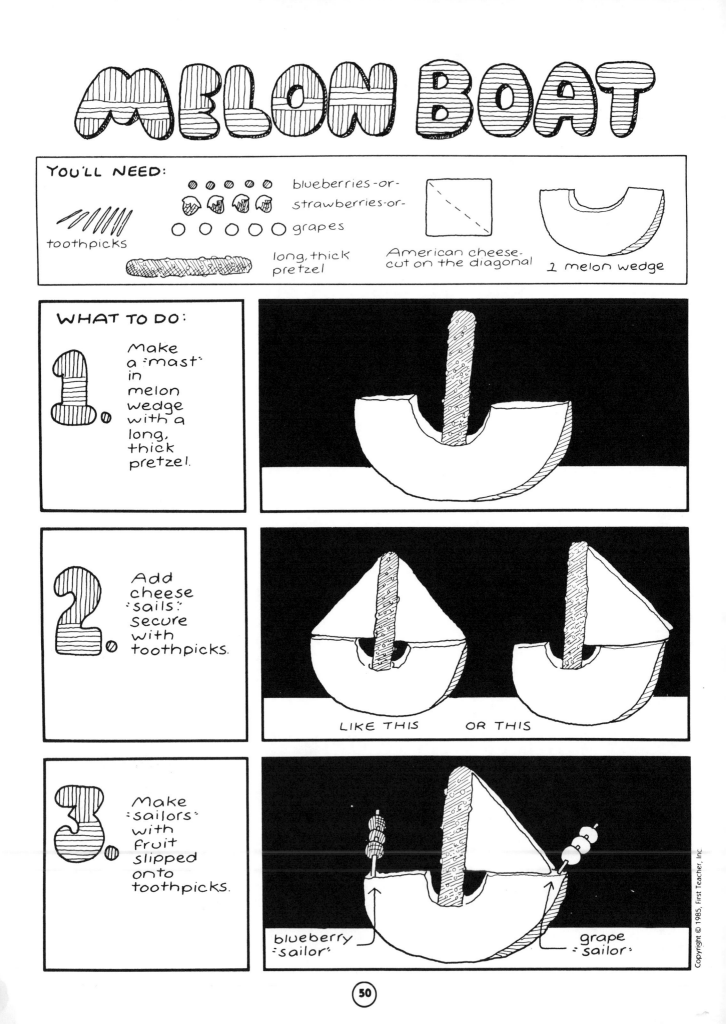

YOU'LL NEED:

toothpicks

blueberries -or- strawberries -or- grapes

long, thick pretzel

American cheese - cut on the diagonal

1 melon wedge

WHAT TO DO:

1. Make a "mast" in melon wedge with a long, thick pretzel.

2. Add cheese "sails." Secure with toothpicks.

LIKE THIS   OR THIS

3. Make "sailors" with fruit slipped onto toothpicks.

blueberry "sailor"

grape "sailor"

50

COLORS

COLORS

Foods present a rainbow of colors that add a special dimension to cooking and eating. The concept of color fits naturally into each cooking experience, as you discuss the colors of the ingredients and how they change through mixing, heating, and cooling. And, the recipes in this chapter are particularly colorful.

Jello-y Jewels

Gelatin desserts have long been favorites of children. This recipe is especially fun because it can be picked up and eaten like candy. Cut the gelatin in cubes, as directed, or use small cookie cutters to make shapes.

If there is an Oriental food store in your area, purchase agar-agar, which is Japanese gelatin, made from seaweed. Follow the directions on the package. Have the children taste it and compare it to Jello-y Jewels.

Purple Cow Shakes

Half the fun of this drink is its name! The other half, of course, is the unusual combination and unique taste of the drink, itself.

Children will enjoy experimenting with other colorful drinks. Let them put together a few of the following suggestions, giving appropriate names to each.

■ Blend pistachio ice cream with milk, and you have a "Green _____." Or, you can combine limeade with lime sherbet.

■ Add strawberry ice cream or sherbet to cranberry juice for a "Red _____." Or, blend strawberry ice cream with milk, and add sparkling, clear soda for a "Pink _____."

■ Blend chocolate ice cream and chocolate milk for a "Brown _____."

Color-fool Foods

These recipes are for your adventurous eaters. Ask children to think about these questions. Does changing the color of the food change its taste? Can you taste the spinach in the green pasta? Does the pink egg taste different from a white one? Have children decide which foods they like best. Make a chart.

Rainbow Cookies

Children love rainbows, and here is an opportunity to make and eat them. Have children observe how the color is kneaded into the dough. They will be able to knead, roll into "snakes," and pat the doughs together. They can even cut the cookies, if they use a plastic knife or wire cheese cutter.

Make a rainbow cake by adding food colors to divided parts of a white cake mix batter. Swirl the colors slightly in the pan. Make rainbow toast by letting children paint diluted food colors on white bread with clean brushes before toasting.

JELLO-Y JEWELS

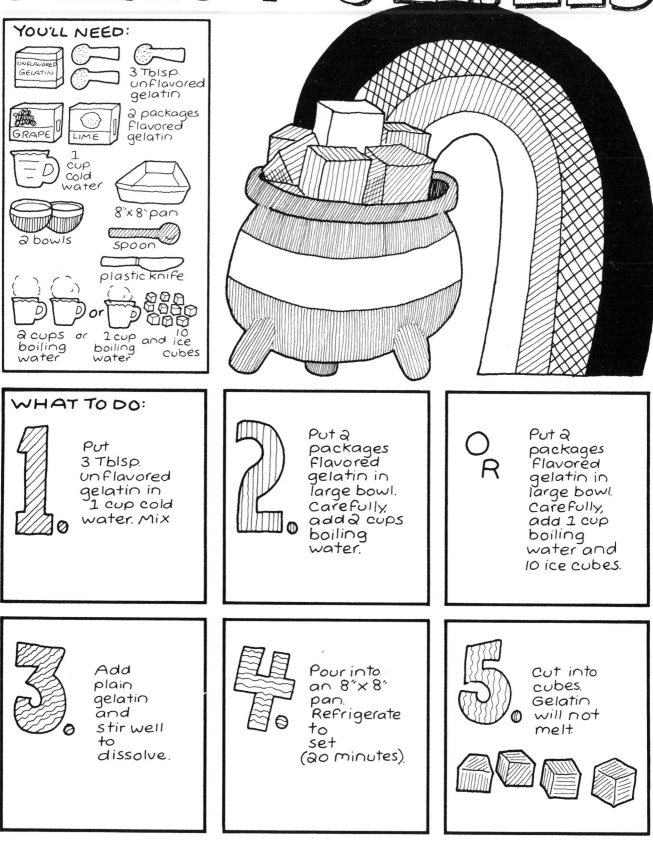

YOU'LL NEED:

UNFLAVORED GELATIN

3 Tblsp. unflavored gelatin

2 packages flavored gelatin

GRAPE   LIME

1 cup cold water

8"x 8" pan

2 bowls

spoon

plastic knife

2 cups boiling water   or   1 cup boiling water   and 10 ice cubes

WHAT TO DO:

1. Put 3 Tblsp. unflavored gelatin in 1 cup cold water. Mix

2. Put 2 packages flavored gelatin in large bowl. Carefully, add 2 cups boiling water.

OR Put 2 packages flavored gelatin in large bowl. Carefully, add 1 cup boiling water and 10 ice cubes.

3. Add plain gelatin and stir well to dissolve.

4. Pour into an 8"x 8" pan. Refrigerate to set (20 minutes).

5. Cut into cubes. Gelatin will not melt.

PURPLE COW SHAKES

YOU'LL NEED:

1 cup milk

1 (6 oz.) can frozen grape juice concentrate

2 cups vanilla ice cream

ice cream scoop

paper cups

blender

drinking straws

"I never saw a purple cow,
I never hope to see one:
But I can tell you, anyhow
I'd rather see than be one."

GELETT BURGESS (1895)

WHAT TO DO:

1. Pour the grape juice concentrate and 1 cup milk into a blender.

2. Scoop in 2 cups vanilla ice cream.

3. Blend for 20 seconds.

4. Sip through straws.

COLOR-FOOL FOODS

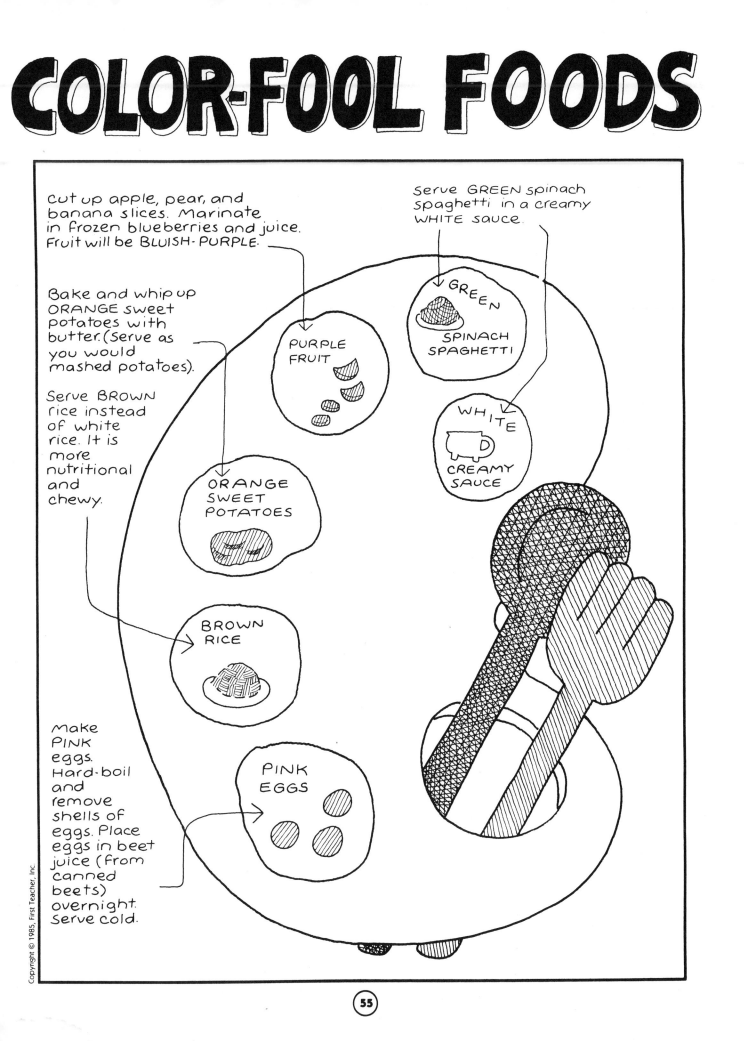

Cut up apple, pear, and banana slices. Marinate in frozen blueberries and juice. Fruit will be BLUISH-PURPLE.

Bake and whip up ORANGE sweet potatoes with butter. (Serve as you would mashed potatoes).

Serve BROWN rice instead of white rice. It is more nutritional and chewy.

Make PINK eggs. Hard-boil and remove shells of eggs. Place eggs in beet juice (from canned beets) overnight. Serve cold.

Serve GREEN spinach spaghetti in a creamy WHITE sauce.

PURPLE FRUIT

GREEN SPINACH SPAGHETTI

WHITE CREAMY SAUCE

ORANGE SWEET POTATOES

BROWN RICE

PINK EGGS

RAINBOW COOKIES

YOU'LL NEED:

- 3½ cups flour
- 2½ tsp. baking powder
- 2 eggs
- 1½ cups sugar
- 1 tsp. vanilla
- 1 tsp. salt
- spoon
- 1 Tblsp. milk
- 2/3 cup shortening
- food coloring- red, yellow, green, blue
- plastic wrap
- bowl
- rolling pin
- plastic knife
- cookie sheet

WHAT TO DO:

1. Mix shortening, sugar, eggs, and vanilla until very fluffy.

2. Add flour mixed with baking powder and salt. Add 1 Tblsp. milk.

3. Mix well and form into ball of dough.

4. Divide and color whole ball of dough as follows:
   1/3 = pink   1/3 = yellow
   and then divide the last 1/3 in half and color 1 blue and 1 green.

5. Knead in color well.

6. Roll blue into a thick log about 8" long.

7. Roll green into a thick log about 8" long. Flatten slightly and place over green log in an arch.

8. Roll yellow into a thick log and flatten. Place, in an arch, over green.

9. Roll pink into a thick log and flatten. Place over yellow.

10. Wrap in plastic wrap and chill 1½- 2 hours.

11. Slice into ¼" pieces.

12. Dip 1 side in granulated sugar.

13. Place sugar side up on a greased cookie sheet. Bake at 400°F for 9 minutes.

pink
yellow
green
blue

SIDE VIEW

green

blue

ARCH

SHAPES

SHAPES

Young children can easily identify the square, circle, and often, the rectangle and triangle. They quickly learn the descriptive words that go along with the shapes, such as *big, small, long*. . . In the recipes that follow, the best part is that children can manipulate the shapes, as they work with them. Use lots of vocabulary to describe the shapes, as children work. After they have had time to experiment, let them make the recipes, as suggested.

Pretzels

To make this pretzel dough, you only need to know two things. First, make sure the warm water is about 110°-115°F. If the water is hotter than 130°F., it will kill the yeast plants. To be exact, use a candy thermometer. Also, make sure you add the sugar (food for the yeast) and just the correct amount of salt. Too much salt will inhibit yeast growth. This recipe makes terrific pretzels, whether you let the dough rise for a while or bake it immediately. You can use the dough to make numbers and letters, as well as shapes. Talk about open and closed shapes, encouraging children to make both.

Homemade Pasta

This recipe helps children realize how one of their favorite foods is made. It also provides a challenge to the child, as he rolls the stiff dough thin. Once this is done, children get to choose what shape macaroni or spaghetti they will make. Talk about wide and narrow, long and short.

Make ravioli and/or lasagna noodles. Prepare them for a meal. Discuss how the same recipe can be made into different shapes, and even folded and filled. Find out which forms of pasta your children like best. Make a graph or chart.

Shortbread Puzzles

This delightful treat is fun to create, assemble, and eat! Children can manage all the preparation from mixing and rolling to pricking and cutting. Try experimenting with various shape puzzles: round, square, and triangular ones. Try cutting out special shapes with cookie cutters, as part of the puzzle.

Make foldout books for the children with six to eight pages. On each page, write one of the action words from this recipe. Include: *rub, add, roll, cut, prick, arrange, brush,* and *bake.* Let children recall, then act out the verb, then draw it on the page with the right word. They each will have a little dictionary-type booklet for future reference.

PRETZELS AND CREATIVE TWISTS

YOU'LL NEED:

1½ cups warm water

1 envelope yeast

4 cups flour

pastry brush

1 tsp. salt

bowls

1 Tblsp. sugar

coarse salt

mixing fork and spoon

WHAT TO DO:

1. Mix together warm water, yeast, sugar. Set aside for 5 minutes.

2. Put salt and flour in a bowl.

3. Add yeast mixture. Mix together to form a dough.

4. Shape dough into creative twists.

5. Beat 1 egg and brush onto twists. Sprinkle on coarse salt.

6. Bake at 425°F for 12 minutes.

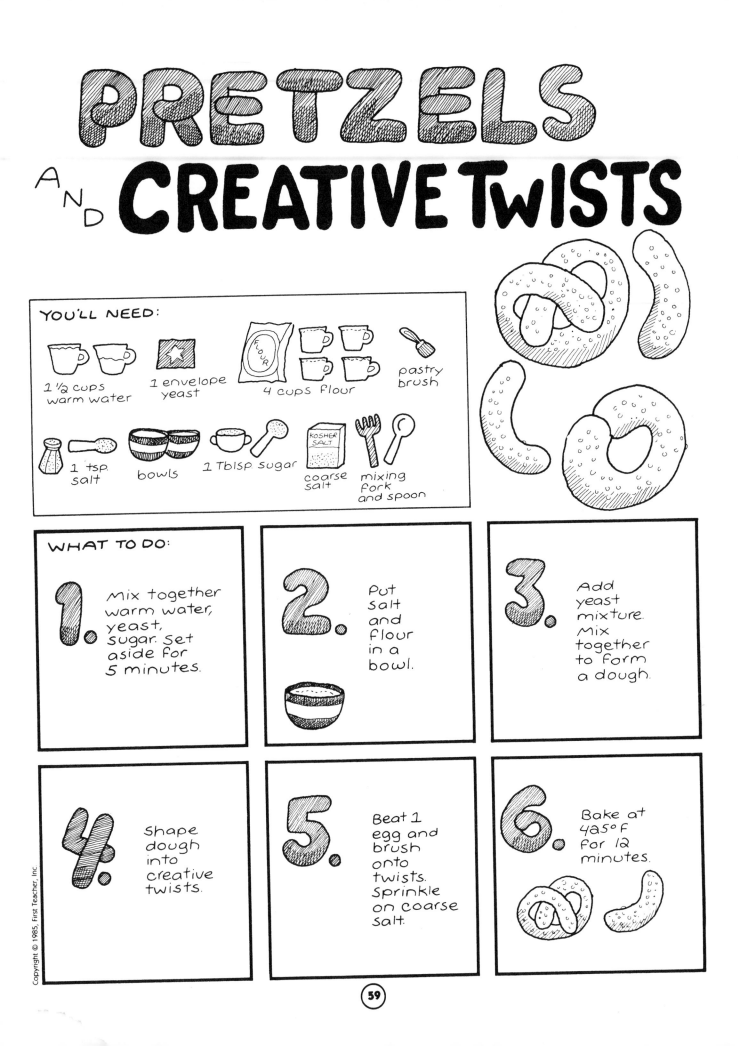

HOMEMADE

YOU'LL NEED:

4 cups flour

2 large eggs

1 egg yolk

2 Tblsp. oil

fork

3/4 cup lukewarm water

knife (ADULT USE ONLY)

plastic wrap

large pot

rolling pin

cookie cutters

bowl

spoon

board or table

strainer

WHAT TO DO:

1. Place 4 cups of flour in center of a board or table. Make a well in the middle.

2. Add eggs and yolk and oil to well. Use a fork to stir flour into eggs. Continue to stir until well-combined.

3. Add water, a little bit at a time, and knead in by hand, adding as much as necessary to make a smooth and elastic dough. Knead about 10 minutes.

4. Let dough rest on the board or table for 30 minutes.

5. Roll 1/2 dough on floured surface to appx 1/8" thick. Stretch and roll again until very thin. Rest a few minutes and then cut..... Keep other 1/2 dough covered in plastic wrap.

6. Adult cuts rolled dough into noodle shapes with a knife. Children can cut small shapes with cookie cutters.

7. Cut pasta can be cooked now in boiling salted water for 4-5 minutes. Drain. Do not rinse.

OR

Cut pasta can be dried completely at room temperature and stored for later use. Sprinkle with a little flour to prevent sticking. Cover and place in freezer. This pasta should be cooked in boiling salted water for 5-6 minutes. Drain. Do not rinse.

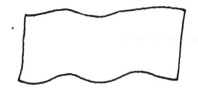

A PASTA
TASTING PARTY

Cook pasta. Drain it and add a Tblsp. of melted butter. Set out a few of the following ingredients to make creative pasta.

grated cheese

tomato sauce

chick peas

tuna chunks

julienne strips of ham, salami, bologna

tomato chunks

herbs: chives, oregano, basil

RAVIOLI

Instead of cutting your rolled pasta dough into noodles, make filled pasta called RAVIOLI.

YOU'LL NEED:

1 recipe pasta dough
2 lbs. ricotta cheese
8 oz. mozzarella cheese
2 eggs
dash- salt, pepper
2 sprigs parsley (optional)
favorite sauce

WHAT TO DO:

1. Mix cheeses, eggs, salt and pepper.

2. Roll dough (1/8" thick) into rectangle.

3. With knife or ravioli cutter, adult cuts 2" squares.

4. Place a heaping tsp. of cheese mixture on square. Top with another square. Prick edges closed with a fork.

5. Place in boiling, salted water. Bring water to boiling again. Boil 15 minutes.

6. Top with your favorite sauce.

LASAGNA

Cut pasta dough into long, wide strips and layer with cheese for LASAGNA.

YOU'LL NEED:

1 recipe pasta dough
3 lbs. ricotta cheese
1/2 cup parmesan cheese
1 lb. mozzarella cheese
2 eggs
2 Tblsp. oil
2 tsp. salt
tomato sauce
dash- salt, pepper

WHAT TO DO:

1. Mix cheeses, eggs, salt, and pepper.

2. Roll dough thin and cut into 12" x 2½" strips. Let dry and cook in boiling water to which 2 Tblsp. oil and 2 tsp. salt have been added. Boil 12-15 minutes.

3. Drain lasagna noodles. Layer noodles, cheese mixture with favorite tomato sauce.

4. Bake at 375°F for 20 minutes or until cooked thoroughly.

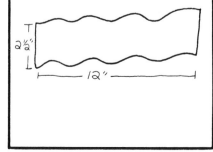

2½"
12"

SHORTBREAD PUZZLES

YOU'LL NEED:

2 cups flour (white or whole wheat)

1/4 cup honey

1/2 cup (1 stick) butter or margarine

bowl

baking sheet

plastic fork and knife

rolling pin

OPTIONAL

1 egg   1 tsp. water   pastry brush

WHAT TO DO:

1. Place flour and butter in a bowl. Rub butter into flour.

2. Add enough honey to moisten into a stiff dough.

3. Use a rolling pin to roll out dough about 3/4" thick. Cut into a rectangular shape.

4. Prick all over with a fork.

5. Use a plastic knife to cut into large puzzle pieces.

6. Arrange on a baking sheet. If desired, brush with a mixture of 1 beaten egg and 1 tsp. water for a glossy look.

7. Bake in a 350° F oven for 20-30 minutes.

MATH

MATH

In cooking, there is lots of obvious math: measuring with cups and spoons; counting, when gathering ingredients; and timing the baking. Children must divide the final product evenly, so they are learning the basics of fractions.

Some math in cooking is more subtle. The following recipes have the obvious math, but each has a little more.

Singing Salad

Children get to count lots of pieces of fruit in this recipe. First, they get to peel, cut, core, chop, and use a melon baller. The whole fruits are broken down into parts. Then, they divide the parts into specific numbers, as they sing the song. And, of course, don't forget the rhythm of the song; it's all math!

This is an excellent recipe to help children learn to estimate. First, figure the amount of individual fruit salads you will need. Then, have the children figure out which fruits you will need the most of. Let them decide how big each piece should be and estimate how many pieces can be cut from one whole fruit. Purchase and use fruit, accordingly. Afterwards, see what is left. How good were the estimates?

Cottage Cheese

The measuring in this recipe is very important. If you add too much vinegar, the cheese will retain the taste. If you add too little, the curds will not form. Beyond the measuring, however, the change occurs in the volume of the final product. Have children observe that you are using two cups of milk to make only about half a cup of cheese. Measure the whey (the liquid you pour off). Do the products add up to the original two cups?

Snacks on a String

Have children help prepare and put out the correct amount of items necessary to make this recipe. Let them count out the pieces, as well as estimate the numbers. Now, have children make patterns with their pieces. This activity comes after children are acquainted with the concept of patterning. Find other patterns. Look at manmade ones on buildings and fabrics. Find patterns in nature on leaves and seashells.

Children also will benefit from the eye-hand coordination it takes to do the stringing. These snacks make great take-alongs.

Sink and Float Jello

Besides measuring and counting the ingredients, children can observe the number of layers in the final product.

Extend this activity by making salad dressing. Use oil and vinegar with herbs and spices. Pour the oil first into a measuring cup to the ⅔ cup line. Then, add ⅓ cup of vinegar and watch them change places. Which one is heavier?

SINGING SALAD

YOU'LL NEED:

apples
bananas
blueberries
plastic knife
melon (watermelon or canteloupe)
paper cups
bowls
melon baller

WHAT TO DO:

1. Prepare and set into separate bowls: melon balls, apple chunks, banana slices, blueberries.

2. For each individual serving, place the following in a cup and sing to the tune of "Ten Little Indians":

: One little, two little, three little, melon balls

four little, five little, six little banana slices

eight little, nine little, apple chunks

ten little blueberries! :

3. Vary the type of fruit used according to the seasons. Change the amounts·but, SING ALONG!

COTTAGE CHEESE

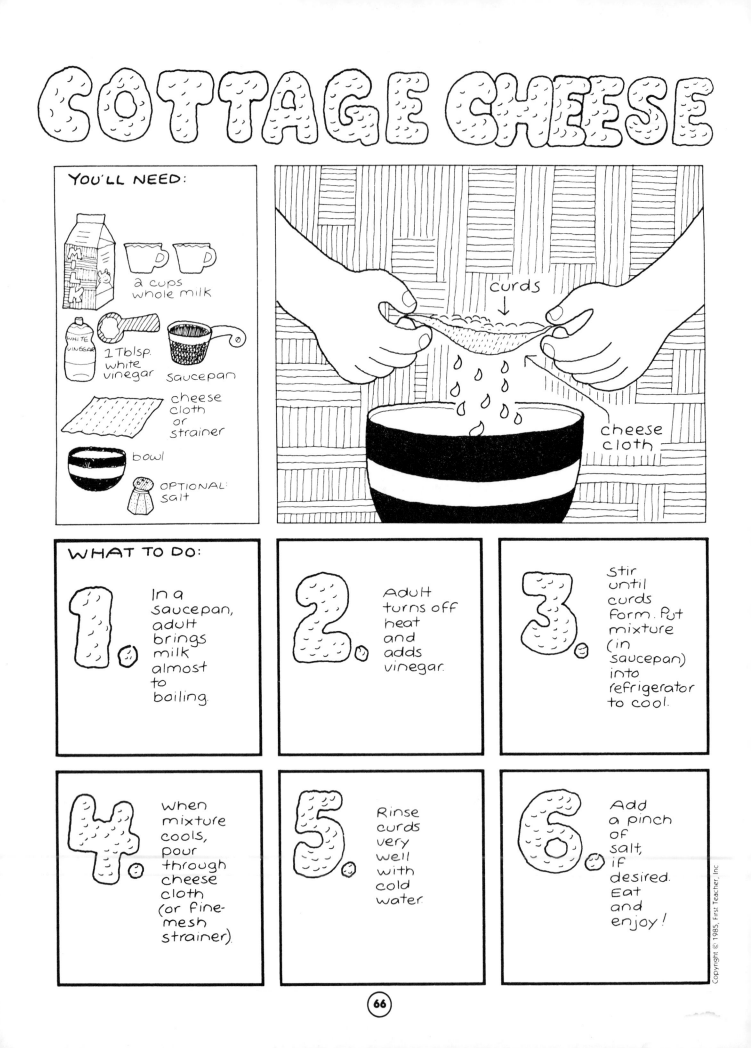

YOU'LL NEED:

2 cups whole milk

1 Tblsp. white vinegar

saucepan

cheese cloth or strainer

bowl

OPTIONAL: salt

curds

cheese cloth

WHAT TO DO:

1. In a saucepan, adult brings milk almost to boiling.

2. Adult turns off heat and adds vinegar.

3. Stir until curds form. Put mixture (in saucepan) into refrigerator to cool.

4. When mixture cools, pour through cheese cloth (or fine-mesh strainer).

5. Rinse curds very well with cold water.

6. Add a pinch of salt, if desired. Eat and enjoy!

SNACKS ON A STRING

YOU'LL NEED:

raisins

cheerios

dried apricots, dried apples, or prunes

large, blunt tapestry needle

popcorn

pretzels

button thread

WHAT TO DO:

1. Set out some or all of the above ingredients in individual bowls.

2. Pick favorite ingredients and set out in a pattern. Use a large, blunt needle and knotted thread to string the foods.

3. Use scissors and cut off needle. Knot ends of string and wear as a necklace. Nibble as needed.

RAISINS

DRIED APPLES

PRETZELS

CHEERIOS

POPCORN

blunt needle

small knot

big knot

SINK AND FLOAT JELL-O

YOU'LL NEED:

FRUIT FLAVOR JELL-O

package of fruit-flavored Jell-O

ASSORTED FRUITS AND FILLINGS (see below)

spoon

clear bowl

water- according to directions

WHAT TO DO:

1. Prepare a package of fruit-flavored Jell-O according to directions. If possible, prepare in a clear bowl.

FRUIT FLAVOR JELL-O

2. When cool, but still liquidy add some or all of the following:

blueberries

mini-marshmallows

sliced banana

sliced peaches -OR- strawberries

grated coconut

grated carrot

chopped walnuts

crushed pineapple

use canned pineapple-packed in its own juice.

CRUSHED PINEAPPLE (in its own juice)

3. Some of these things will float. Some will sink. Talk about why things sink or float.

Chill Jell-O. Eat and see layers of fruit and Jell-O. Make a chart about things that stay up (float) and things that go to the bottom (sink).

mini-marshmallows

grated coconut

Jell-O

crushed pineapple

LANGUAGE DEVELOPMENT

LANGUAGE DEVELOPMENT

With any cooking experience, children are learning new vocabulary words, as they observe foods with all of their senses and perform the operations that illustrate action words.

They are also developing language skills by following the sequence of steps in a recipe. And, you can ask them to review the steps and recall details, as you enjoy the final product.

Jack Be Nimble and Humpty Dumpty Egg

These are two of those "easy to put together" recipes. Children can assemble one of their very own, as they recite the Mother Goose rhymes:

"Jack be nimble, Jack be quick.
Jack jumped over the candlestick."

"Humpty Dumpty sat on the wall.
Humpty Dumpty had a great fall.
All the king's horses and all the king's men
Couldn't put Humpty together again."

Mother Goose rhymes have a lively rhythm and catchy sound to the words and verses. They should be used frequently with young children. See how many other nursery rhymes you might accompany with a cooking experience. Try *"Little Miss Muffett"* and the recipe for cottage cheese on page 66. It makes curds and whey. Make a pie for Simple Simon.

Play Foods

These take a little effort to make, but are so well worth it! Children get to use their observation and recall skills. They can tell you that the hot dog goes IN the bun and the berries go INSIDE the crust; the meatballs go ON TOP OF the spaghetti. They use descriptive and directional words, as they create each food item.

After the play foods are constructed, baked, and painted, they can be used in the dramatic play area. Here, children will use them to "prepare" meals and play restaurant. When they are playing restaurant, be sure to hand the waiter or waitress a pad and pencil to "scribble write" the order.

PLEASE NOTE: Use these play foods with children five years and older. Younger children may attempt to put them in their mouths. You can leave the play foods unpainted and without the polyurethane cover for four year olds. However, some very young children probably still will try to chew them. Use under proper supervision.

JACK BE NIMBLE
CANDLESTICK

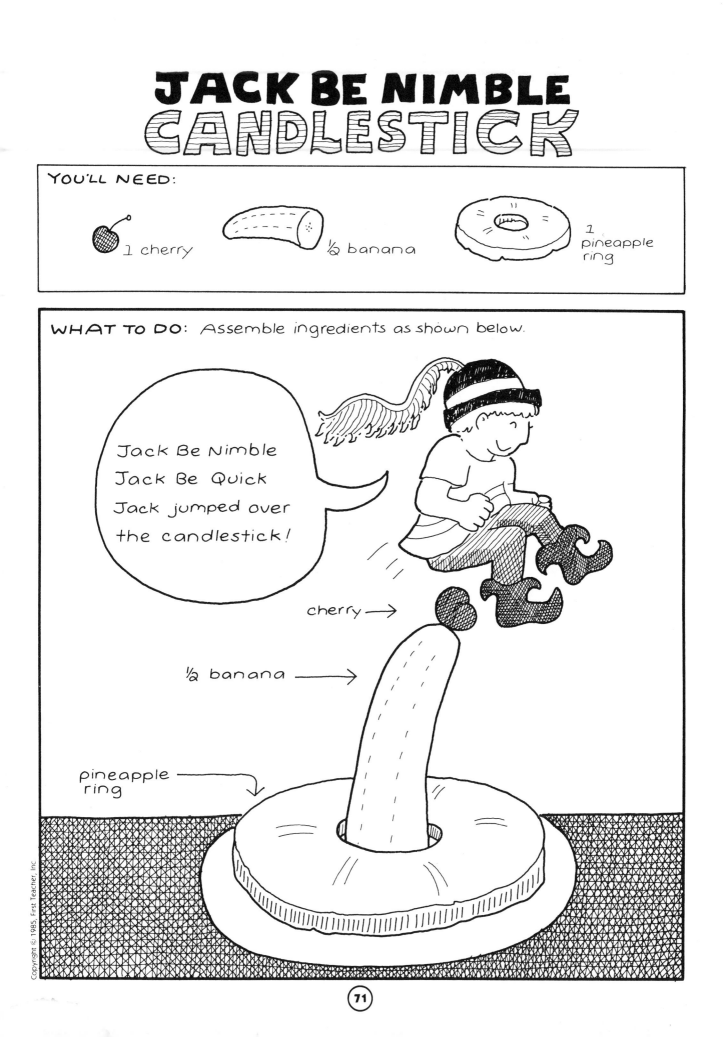

YOU'LL NEED:

1 cherry   ½ banana   1 pineapple ring

WHAT TO DO: Assemble ingredients as shown below.

Jack Be Nimble
Jack Be Quick
Jack jumped over
the candlestick!

cherry →

½ banana →

pineapple ring →

PLAY FOODS

YOU'LL NEED:

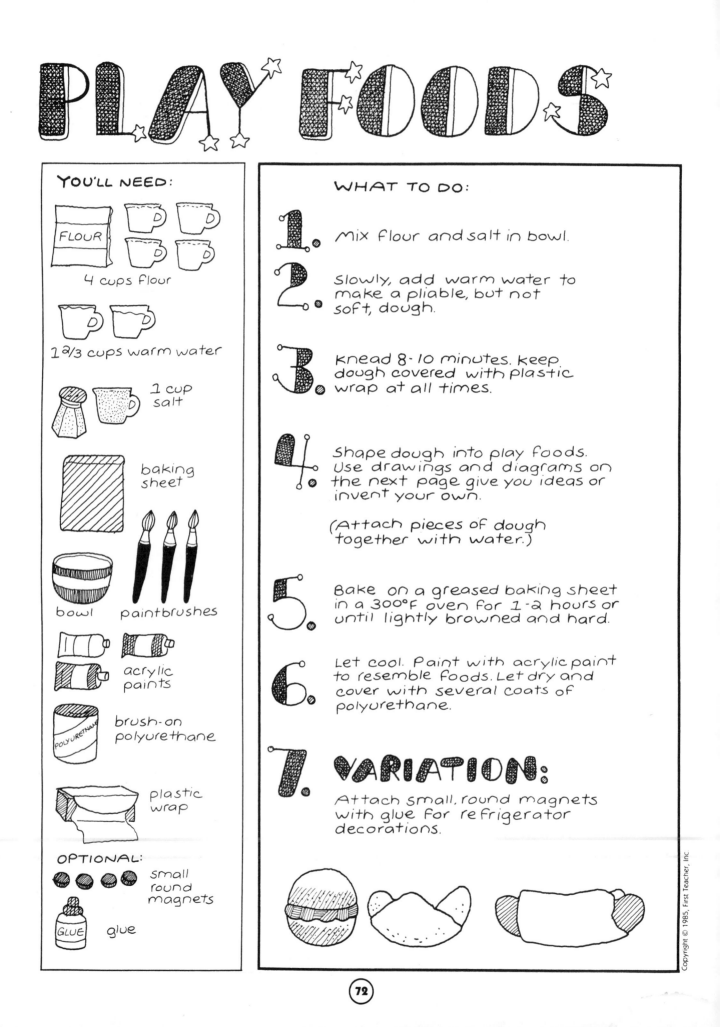

FLOUR

4 cups flour

1 2/3 cups warm water

1 cup salt

baking sheet

bowl   paintbrushes

acrylic paints

brush-on polyurethane

plastic wrap

OPTIONAL:

small round magnets

GLUE   glue

WHAT TO DO:

1. Mix flour and salt in bowl.

2. Slowly, add warm water to make a pliable, but not soft, dough.

3. Knead 8-10 minutes. keep dough covered with plastic wrap at all times.

4. Shape dough into play foods. Use drawings and diagrams on the next page give you ideas or invent your own.

(Attach pieces of dough together with water.)

5. Bake on a greased baking sheet in a 300°F oven for 1-2 hours or until lightly browned and hard.

6. Let cool. Paint with acrylic paint to resemble foods. Let dry and cover with several coats of polyurethane.

7. ## VARIATION:

Attach small, round magnets with glue for refrigerator decorations.

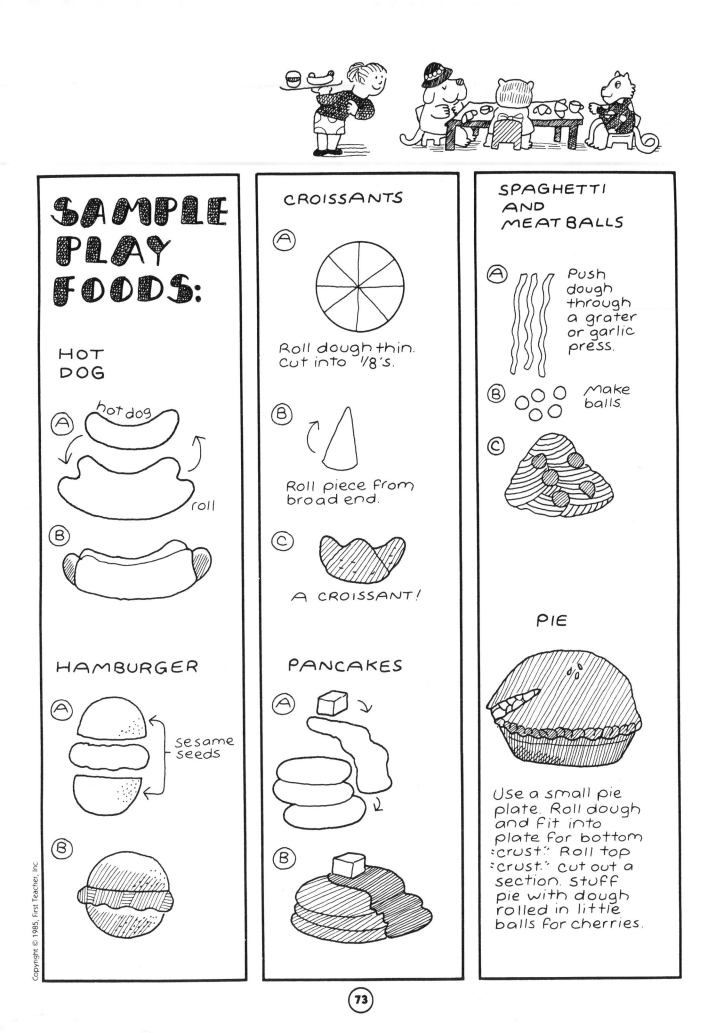

SAMPLE PLAY FOODS:

HOT DOG

(A) hot dog
roll

(B)

HAMBURGER

(A) sesame seeds

(B)

CROISSANTS

(A) Roll dough thin. Cut into 1/8's.

(B) Roll piece from broad end.

(C) A CROISSANT!

PANCAKES

(A)

(B)

SPAGHETTI AND MEATBALLS

(A) Push dough through a grater or garlic press.

(B) Make balls.

(C)

PIE

Use a small pie plate. Roll dough and fit into plate for bottom "crust." Roll top "crust." Cut out a section. Stuff pie with dough rolled in little balls for cherries.

HUMPTY DUMPTY EGG

YOU'LL NEED:

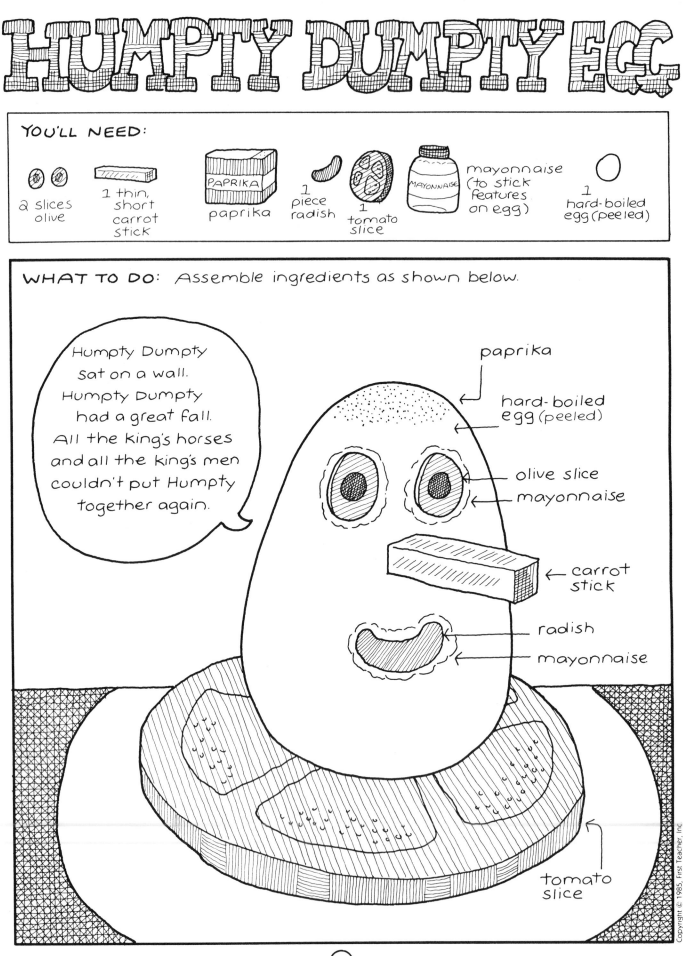

2 slices olive

1 thin, short carrot stick

paprika

1 piece radish

1 tomato slice

mayonnaise (to stick features on egg)

1 hard-boiled egg (peeled)

WHAT TO DO: Assemble ingredients as shown below.

Humpty Dumpty sat on a wall. Humpty Dumpty had a great fall. All the king's horses and all the king's men couldn't put Humpty together again.

paprika

hard-boiled egg (peeled)

olive slice

mayonnaise

carrot stick

radish

mayonnaise

tomato slice

SCIENCE

SCIENCE

Your kitchen is really a laboratory! You can demonstrate very simple scientific principles by making ice cubes from frozen water and making steam from boiling water. Combine baking soda and vinegar for oodles of bubbles. Demonstrate what heat does to foods. Use every opportunity to bring out the science in your cooking activities.

"Grow It Again"

Growing plants helps children learn about the origins of foods. By growing plants from parts of leftovers, children get to see how the vegetable was first used, and then, where the seed came from to grow more of the same type of plant. Some of the "Grow It Again" vegetables, like carrot tops, will only make plant growth and not bear fruit. Seeds for new vegetables will grow only from the greenery.

Basic to this activity is a respect for nature. Instead of just discarding the unused part of the plant, we are recycling it into something useful, or, at least a thing of beauty.

Butter

Today, most children drink milk from plastic or paper containers and wonder where it comes from. Use pictures to show the route of milk, from the farm to the consumer. Talk about all the products we get from milk.

Butter, also can be made by whipping cream until it is very thick. The shaking method, however, is much more similar to the old fashioned butter churn, with the marble acting as the churn.

Yogurt

Yogurt is made when bacteria multiply in warm milk. Although children cannot see the bacteria multiplying, they see the results of the action. Heat makes this process happen. Explain to the children that many things in nature cannot be seen, but we can see the things that they do.

Again, change has occurred when the liquid becomes a semisolid. Have children taste the yogurt and compare it to the taste of fresh milk. They will probably think it is sour. Let them add fruits or jams, if they wish.

Jumping Raisins

Demonstrate to children how juicy, round grapes become dried, wrinkled raisins. Heat causes the evaporation of the moisture in the grapes. Dry other fruits and vegetables. Slice pears and peaches very thin, dip into lemon juice, and spread on a basket or screen outside in the sun. Cover with cheesecloth and allow to dry for a few days. Compare the dried fruit to moist fruit. Weigh two pieces. Talk about the difference in weight.

GROW IT AGAIN!

Eat these vegetables and fruits and use different parts to grow new plants.

CITRUS TREE

Plant orange, grapefruit, or lemon seed ½" deep in soil.

It will take several weeks to sprout.

ONION

Find an onion that is already sprouted. Plant in soil.

TURNIP

Cut pointed end from turnip. Scoop out, leaving sides about ½" thick. Hang in a sunny window and keep filled with water.

PINEAPPLE

Cut off the top and trim 3 rows of bottom leaves. Let dry for 3 days. Plant 1" deep in soil. Keep moist and sunny.

AVOCADO

Set large end of avocado seed in jar of water, using 3 toothpicks. Sprout in partial sunlight. When the stem is about 4"-5" tall. Plant in soil.

CARROT

Cut off top and trim off all leaves. Place in a layer of pebbles in a flat dish. Keep well-watered.

BUTTER

YOU'LL NEED:

2 cups heavy cream

wooden spoon

glass marble

plastic container with lid

small bowl

WHAT TO DO:

1.

Put cream into container. Add marble. Cover tightly and shake.

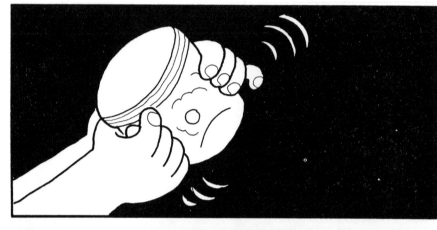

2.

In about 15 minutes, the butter should separate from the thin, white liquid (buttermilk). Press out all liquid with a wooden spoon. Remove marble.

3.

Chill butter. Taste. (It will be sweet.) Add a pinch of salt, if desired.

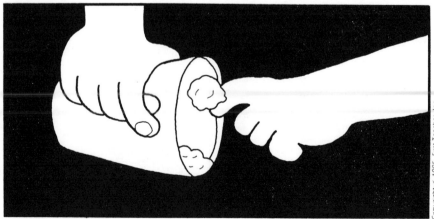

YOGURT

YOU'LL NEED:

3 Tblsp. plain yogurt

water

1 large can evaporated milk

covered bowl

spoon

½ tsp. unflavored gelatin

POWDERED MILK

3 cups powdered milk

paper cups

slice

OPTIONAL:
Fruit-
blueberries
strawberries
banana

WHAT TO DO:

1. Soften gelatin in a small amount of cold water.

2. Add boiling water to make 1 cup. Cool.

3. Preheat oven to 275° F. Mix 3 cups dry milk with 3 cups water in a large bowl.

4. Add evaporated milk, 2 more cups of lukewarm water, and the gelatin mixture.

5. Add 3 Tblsp. yogurt. Stir thoroughly.

6. Cover the bowl. Put covered bowl in oven and turn it off.

7. Leave covered bowl in turned-off oven for 8-10 hours.

8. Refrigerate when done. ☆

☆ when chilled, add fruit, if desired.

paper cup ↵

JUMPING RAISINS

YOU'LL NEED:

½-1 lb. fresh green grapes

dish or flat basket

paper towels

CLUB SODA, lemon soda — club soda, seltzer, or lemon soda

tall, clear glass

spoon

WHAT TO DO:

1. Wash and dry with paper towels ½-1 lb. fresh green grapes.

2. Place grapes in a dish or flat basket in a sunny, warm place.

3. In nice weather, grapes will become raisins in a few days. If you place near a sunny window, it will take a little longer.

4. When grapes have dried into raisins make JUMPING RAISINS.....

5. Pour club soda, seltzer, or lemon soda into a tall, clear glass. Add 4-6 raisins. Observe. Raisins will sink to the bottom, then slowly rise to the top. They will continue to jump up and down for several minutes.

6. Wait until all the raisins settle to the bottom of the glass, then drink the soda. Get the raisins out with a spoon and eat!

CHILDREN'S LITERATURE

CHILDREN'S LITERATURE

Do you remember:
- Hansel and Gretel nibbling on the witch's gingerbread house?
- the farmer and his wife and the cow running after the gingerbread boy?
- the townspeople huddled around a kettle of soup made from a stone?

Many famous scenes from classic children's books can be enjoyed, not only for their creativity, humor, and often sensitivity, but also as starting points for fun and learning when combined with a cooking experience.

Currant Buns

The tale of Peter Rabbit is one of the most popular stories in children's literature. This recipe ties in with the currant buns Mrs. Rabbit was going off to buy when she sent Flopsy, Mopsy, Cotton-tail, and Peter to pick blackberries. Use this recipe to do some creative dramatics. Set up a tea party with real tea and currant buns. Have the children take the parts in the story.

Big Batch of Gingerbread

Children delight in the familiar story and its catchy refrain "Run, run, as fast as you can. . . You can't catch me, I'm the Gingerbread Man." Let them make the gingerbread boy and decorate him with icing and raisins. Use this dough to make freeform characters from the whole story.

This recipe can be used to make tree decorations at holiday time. Roll the dough to ½ inch and cut with cookie cutters. Poke a hole at the top of the uncooked dough and bake.

The Perfect Pancake

Let children become creative chefs when they use this recipe. They can mix the batter, then use the additional ingredients to make their own perfect pancake. Let them make one to eat right away and one to put on display and then share with others.

Make a pancake cookbook. Take a picture of each pancake and its creator. If you cannot take photos, have each child draw his creation. Bind the papers together. On the first page, write the basic recipe. On succeeding pages, have each child describe his additions to go along with his picture.

Pumpkin Seeds

The pumpkin is a fantastic teaching tool. Besides being a nutritious vegetable and a festive Jack O'Lantern, you can bake it, scrap it, and use the pulp for muffins, breads, pies, or even soup. You can cut a raw pumpkin into thin slices, dry them and eat them like candy. And, the best part is still available — the seeds! After completing this recipe, if you have leftover raw seeds, you can soak them for half an hour in warm water and let older children use a needle and thread to make a seed necklace.

CURRANT BUNS ☆

YOU'LL NEED:

- 1 cup warm milk (115°F)
- 1 envelope yeast
- 1 tsp. salt
- ¼ cup currants
- 1 Tblsp. sugar
- spoon
- 2 Tblsp. butter
- bowl
- 2½ cups (or more) flour

☆ PETER RABBIT
by Beatrix Potter

WHAT TO DO:

1. Combine milk and yeast.

2. Add butter, sugar, salt, and flour to yeast/milk mixture. Mix well.

3. Knead for 8 minutes. Let rise in a warm place in a greased bowl for 1 hour.

4. Add currants and form dough into little balls.

5. Let rise 1 hour.

6. Bake at 425°F for 15 minutes.

BIG BATCH OF GINGERBREAD

☆ THE GINGERBREAD BOY

YOU'LL NEED:

2/3 cup water · 1 1/2 cups molasses · 1/4 tsp. cinnamon · 1/4 tsp. nutmeg · 1/4 tsp. ginger

1/3 cup shortening · 1 cup brown sugar · 1 tsp. salt · spoon · 2 tsp. baking soda · bowl · cookie sheet · raisins · nuts · 6 cups (or more) flour

WHAT TO DO:

1. Combine sugar, shortening, molasses.

2. Mix all dry ingredients together.

3. Add dry ingredients to moist ingredients. Mix.

4. Roll or pat out gingerbread people.

5. Decorate with raisins and nuts.

6. Bake at 350°F for 15 minutes on a greased cookie sheet.

PANCAKES

☆ THE PERFECT PANCAKE by *Virginia Kahl* and PANCAKES, PANCAKES by *Eric Carle*

YOU'LL NEED:

2 eggs, beaten
½ tsp. salt
griddle
baking powder 1¼ tsp.
1⅓ cups milk
2 tsp. sugar
FLOUR 1⅓ cups flour
3 Tblsp. melted butter or oil
egg beater
CREATIVE PART AND TOPPINGS· see below

WHAT TO DO:

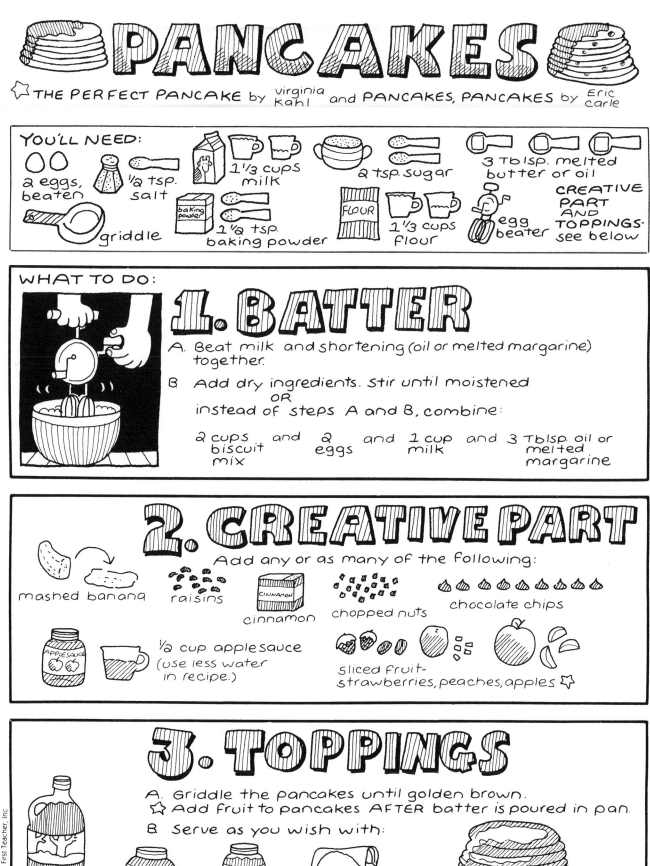

1. BATTER

A. Beat milk and shortening (oil or melted margarine) together.

B. Add dry ingredients. Stir until moistened

OR

instead of steps A and B, combine:

2 cups biscuit mix   and   2 eggs   and   1 cup milk   and   3 Tblsp. oil or melted margarine

2. CREATIVE PART

Add any or as many of the following:

mashed banana
raisins
CINNAMON cinnamon
chopped nuts
chocolate chips
¼ cup applesauce (use less water in recipe.)
sliced fruit- strawberries, peaches, apples ☆

3. TOPPINGS

A. Griddle the pancakes until golden brown.
☆ Add fruit to pancakes AFTER batter is poured in pan.

B. Serve as you wish with:

syrup- maple or blueberry
applesauce
HONEY honey
rolled up with fruit or cottage cheese
spread with cream cheese or peanut butter

PUMPKIN SEEDS

☆PUMPKIN SEEDS by Steven Yezback

YOU'LL NEED:

paper towels — pumpkin — salt — OIL oil — frying pan — knife (ADULT USE ONLY)

WHAT TO DO:

1. Adult cuts open a pumpkin.

2. separate seeds from stringy membrane.

3. Wash seeds. Drain and dry on paper towels.

4. Adult heats oil in frying pan.

5. Carefully, place pumpkin seeds into pan and fry until almost golden-colored.

6. Drain pumpkin seeds on paper towels and salt lightly.

7. Eat, while seeds still are warm.

OPPOSITES

OPPOSITES

Children become aware of opposites by first observing the similarities in things. Once they know the characteristics of something, they can know what the opposite will be. These recipes present various types of opposites — hot/cold, hard/soft, sweet/sour, and liquid/solid. Use descriptive vocabulary, while preparing them. Let children describe the changes they see, in their own words.

–Sicles

These icy cold treats can be made in so many ways. Experiment with fruit juices for good nutrition and milk products for more protein. Compare the textures of the various –sicles.

For more fun with freezing, make ice cubes for drinks with fruit juices, or add cherries, berries, and tiny pieces of fruit to clear water in trays for pretty cubes. Place half a banana on a –sicle stick. Set in the freezer, until hard. Roll in melted chocolate bits, and then in crisp rice cereal. The unusual contrast is delicious. Freeze grapes for a different taste and texture for older children. Talk about each of these projects in terms of solid/liquid, hard/soft, hot/cold.

Cold Spaghetti Salad

Most children love spaghetti, and most are used to eating it hot with sauce or butter. Have a hot spaghetti day. Talk about the dry spaghetti from the box (or homemade spaghetti, described on page 60). Note that it is hard, thin, and breaks easily. Examine a cooked piece. It is the opposite — soft, thicker, and bendable. Serve with a hot sauce or melted butter and cheese. Then, have a cold spaghetti day. Cook the spaghetti and cool. Follow the recipe. Talk about the unexpected tastes and textures.

Sweet/Sour Pickles

Sweet and sour is a classic taste treat. Much Oriental cooking is based on the idea of combining these opposite, yet complementary, tastes.

Along with this recipe, have a tasting party. Include some naturally sweet foods, such as apples, strawberries, bananas, and some sour foods, such as pickles and lemons. Let children describe the tastes.

Maple Candy

This very easy recipe demonstrates a number of opposites. The liquid syrup is boiled, until it is soft and pliable; then, it becomes hard and brittle, when poured over ice. Children delight in watching the hot liquid become almost instantly cold, when it touches ice.

-SICLES

JUICE AND MILK AND YOGURT -SICLES

YOU'LL NEED:

5 oz. paper cups

plastic spoons - 1 per cup

PUNCH **OR** CHOCOLATE MILK **OR** OJ

fruit punch **or** chocolate milk **or** reconstituted orange juice

WHAT TO DO:

1. choose 1 type of '-sicle' to make: orange, chocolate milk, or fruit punch.

2. Pour orange juice, chocolate milk, or fruit punch into cups.

3. Freeze about 1 hour and then add plastic spoon to the center.

spoons

5. Freeze until solid.

6. Peel away cup.

COLD SPAGHETTI SALAD

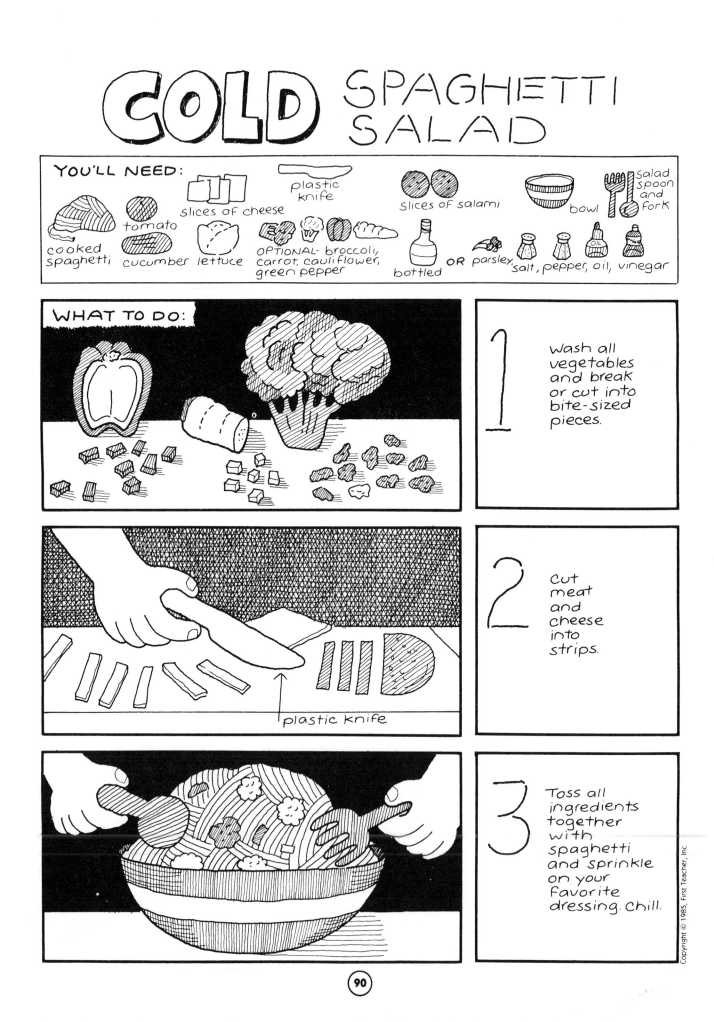

YOU'LL NEED:

plastic knife

slices of cheese

slices of salami

bowl

salad spoon and fork

tomato

cooked spaghetti

cucumber   lettuce

OPTIONAL- broccoli, carrot, cauliflower, green pepper

bottled   OR   parsley, salt, pepper, oil, vinegar

WHAT TO DO:

plastic knife

1 — Wash all vegetables and break or cut into bite-sized pieces.

2 — Cut meat and cheese into strips.

3 — Toss all ingredients together with spaghetti and sprinkle on your favorite dressing. Chill.

SWEET/SOUR PICKLES

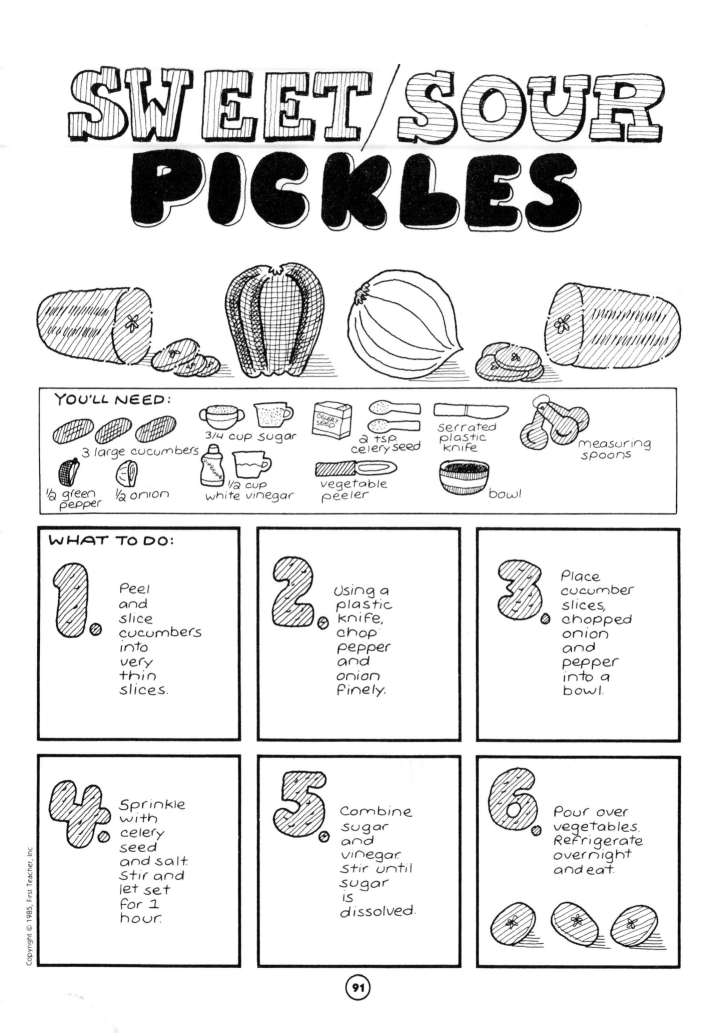

YOU'LL NEED:

3 large cucumbers

3/4 cup sugar

CELERY SEED — 2 tsp. celery seed

serrated plastic knife

measuring spoons

1/2 green pepper

1/2 onion

VINEGAR — 1/2 cup white vinegar

vegetable peeler

bowl

WHAT TO DO:

1. Peel and slice cucumbers into very thin slices.

2. Using a plastic knife, chop pepper and onion finely.

3. Place cucumber slices, chopped onion and pepper into a bowl.

4. Sprinkle with celery seed and salt. Stir and let set for 1 hour.

5. Combine sugar and vinegar. Stir until sugar is dissolved.

6. Pour over vegetables. Refrigerate overnight and eat.

MAPLE CANDY

YOU'LL NEED:

MAPLE SYRUP

½ cup maple syrup or maple blend syrup

13" x 9" baking pan

saucepan

water

WHAT TO DO:

1. Fill baking pan 3/4 of way full with water.

2. Freeze until solid.

3. Adult brings syrup to boil and boils for 7 minutes.

4. Slowly, pour hot syrup in long strips over ice. It will harden to maple candy.

5. Remove from ice and eat.

NOTE: The candy will be like soft taffy if boiled slightly less than 7 minutes. Test to make sure it is hard candy.

CELEBRATIONS

CELEBRATIONS

Celebrations are those wonderful breaks in the regular routine that allow us to enjoy traditional holidays or recognize special achievements or people. Celebrations mean different foods, fun activities, and good times! They don't necessarily have to be big, elaborate parties. In fact, the best celebrations are those that the children help to plan and prepare. Then, the festivities become a real learning situation.

There are often special foods associated with holiday celebrations. For example, gingerbread boys (See the recipe on page 84.) just go naturally with Christmas, as potato pancakes go with Hanukkah. Something orange for Halloween is a necessity. (See the Jack O'Lantern Fruit Salad on page 37.) The spring recipes in this book make great alternatives to sweeter Easter treats.

Birthdays are holidays that we all get to celebrate once a year. Use the special recipes in this chapter for unusual birthday party foods.

Other celebrations are very specialized. They only have meaning to a small, intimate group. They often come as a joyful surprise. Celebrate the special events in the lives of your children, like the first lost tooth, a new brother or sister, a new pet, or even new achievements like being able to ride a bike or tie one's own shoes. Never pass up the opportunity to make a child feel important. And, of course, use the little celebration to interject some learning.

The following recipes range from sweet, very special treats like Cake 'N Ice Cream, to more natural and unusual celebration foods like the Apple from Outer Space and Orange Sipper. You must be the judge of what is acceptable for each group and occasion.

Celebration Bread

Although this is not a traditional holiday treat, children will enjoy eating it and making it because they can really get their hands into it — literally. This recipe has all the advantages of using doughs with children: the practice in motor coordination, eye-hand coordination, working with a material that takes a creative form. . . The children will be delighted with the process!

The basic white bread recipe is very nearly perfect. I've used it hundreds of times with children; and, it has never failed. Just remember to treat the yeast with respect Use fresh packets of yeast and dissolve in water 110° to 115°F. Use a candy thermometer to test the warm water. As you set the yeast and water aside for the allotted three minutes, add ½ tsp. of sugar to it. If the yeast is growing properly, it will start to bubble and foam. If it doesn't, something is wrong with the yeast. Discard.

Cake 'N Ice Cream

This variation on the traditional party food is fun to assemble, as well as a surprise to eat. Children enjoy pulling chunks of soft cake from the well you've cut, and, then, stuffing it with softened ice cream, ice milk, or frozen yogurt.

You might want to consider making other cake and ice cream specialties. Try individual cakes, baked in an ice cream cone and topped with a scoop of ice cream. Prepare cake batter and pour into flat bottomed ice cream cones. Set on a cookie sheet and bake, as you would a cupcake. Cool and add the ice cream.

Orange Sipper

Nothing beats the taste of freshly squeezed orange juice; yet, often, it is too difficult or messy for young children. This recipe takes care of these problems. The children get to push, punch, and press the half orange, and then, sip the delicious juice.

Try other zip locking bag treats for celebrations. Make instant pudding in a bag with one package pudding, ⅔ cup of dried milk, and 1¾ cup of water, added right before you are ready to zip it closed and shake, shake, shake. Open one corner and squeeze into an ice cream cone.

Apple from Outer Space

Children will have a great time poking holes into the apple and sticking pretzels in them. The recipe is a party in itself! It is also a nutritious alternative to traditional party foods.

Consider using other healthy foods for celebrations. If you make them special, include the children in their preparation, and serve them just right, they will be a hit. Use fruits, cheeses, peanut butter, and vegetables.

Racers

Although made with nothing sweeter than raisins, this creative put together will become a party favorite for your older children. You can set the ingredients out to limit the choices, yet allow for individual creations. Show children the examples, suggest alternative parts, and let them go. Before everyone eats, have a little car racer show.

Corn Doggies

Celebration foods often mean taking the usual ingredients, adding something a little different, and serving the food with a flair. In corn doggies, the everyday hot dog gets a hearty cornmeal crust, is served up on a stick, and becomes an instant party treat.

Children can help in all stages of preparation: the mixing, the sticking, and the dipping. You must do the frying.

Pigs in Blankets

This recipe makes the hot dog fun to prepare and special to eat. Watch out for one thing; the name may be misleading to your children. One little girl actually thought she would have to eat a pig in a blanket. This is another good reason for children to cook: they see the ingredients in dishes with unusual names.

Very young children may have difficulty eating hot dogs. They may gag or choke on them particularly if they are cut into round slices. Leave hot dogs for the four and five year old group.

Fortune Cookies

This recipe is lots of fun and takes only 20 minutes to prepare. You are also combining language arts with a cooking experience. You and the children can write all sorts of messages or draw cute pictures on the paper strips to put inside.

The cookies themselves are tastier than the restaurant variety. You must fry each cookie and let it cool slightly before children handle it. Crisp the cookies in the oven before serving.

CELEBRATION BREAD

YOU'LL NEED:

2 packages yeast

3/4 cup warm water (115° F)

2 Tblsp. sugar or honey

4 1/2 - 5 1/2 cups flour (white or mixed with a little whole wheat)

1 1/4 cups buttermilk

4 Tblsp. margarine

2 tsp. baking powder

2 tsp. salt

bowls

mixing spoon

waxed paper

cookie sheet

OR

2 loaf pans

BASIC RECIPE

WHAT TO DO:

 1. Combine yeast and warm water. Set aside for 3 minutes.

 2. In a bowl, combine 4 1/2 cups flour, sugar, salt, baking powder, and margarine. Mix well.

3. Add yeast mixture to bowl.

 4. Slowly add buttermilk and stir well. Dough should be soft but not sticky.

 5. Knead 8 minutes.

 6. Grease a cookie sheet or 2 loaf pans. Place dough in pans or shape on a cookie sheet.

 7. Grease a large piece of waxed paper and cover dough. Let rise in a warm place for 45 minutes.

8. Remove waxed paper and place dough in preheated 400° F oven for 20- 40 minutes. (20 minutes- for small shaped loaves; 35-40 minutes for pan loaves.)

Great with a THANKSGIVING DINNER!

VARIATIONS

CHRISTMAS

knead into basic recipe:

½ CUP NUTS (PINE NUTS are great)

½ CUP RED and GREEN GLACEED CHERRIES

¼ CUP SOFT RAISINS

CHANNUKAH

Shape bread dough into 3 balls. Roll each out long. Braid. Before baking, glaze with beaten EGG WHITE and 1 tsp WATER. Sprinkle with POPPY SEED.

VALENTINE'S DAY

Shape dough into 2 hearts on baking sheets. Bake and then glaze with POWDERED MILK FROSTING:

1. Cream 2 Tblsp. BUTTER and ⅓ CUP HONEY. Add 1 Tblsp. MILK and 1 tsp. VANILLA.

2. Blend in ¾ cup POWDERED MILK (POWDER).

3. Add more MILK (liquid or dry) for right consistency.

ST. PATRICK'S DAY

Take ⅓ of dough and knead in GREEN FOOD COLORING. Divide rest of dough into 3 large balls and 1 small ball. Press some green dough on each ball. Twist or press doughs together. Do not mix heavily. Shape balls into a SHAMROCK on a greased baking sheet. Bake.

EASTER

Shape dough into 3 balls. Roll each out long. Braid and shape braid into a circle. Dye RAW EGGS in Easter dyes. Place 4 or 5 eggs IN raised braid. Bake in oven for 35-45 minutes. Cool. Glaze with CONFECTIONER'S SUGAR and MILK combined. Sprinkle with pastel NONPAREILS.

CAKE 'N ICE CREAM

YOU'LL NEED:

1 angel food or other type tube shaped cake

1 pint ice cream

1 package instant vanilla pudding

1/4 cup confectionary sugar

1 cup cold milk

1 regular size container Cool Whip

mixer and bowl

spoon

knife (ADULT USE ONLY)

WHAT TO DO:

1. Adult cuts off top 1/4 of cake (Save cake top for later.)

2. Cut a well in cake, leaving 1/2" all around. Scoop out cake with a spoon.

3. Fill well in cake with ice cream.

ice cream

4. Replace top on cake.

MAKE FROSTING:

5. ⓐ Mix pudding, cold milk, and sugar. Beat 1 minute. Let set for 2 minutes.

ⓑ Fold in Cool Whip

6. Frost cake and place in freezer.

Frosting

ORANGE SIPPER

YOU'LL NEED:

½ orange (no seeds)

1 drinking straw

1 sandwich size zip locking plastic bag.

WHAT TO DO:

1. Place ½ orange in a plastic bag. Squeeze out most of the air.

2. Seal plastic bag. Squeeze orange to get out juice.

3. Open a corner slightly. Place straw inside and drink.

APPLE FROM OUTER SPACE

YOU'LL NEED:

stick pretzels

small cheese cubes

apple

fork

WHAT TO DO:

1. Use the fork to poke holes in the apple.

2. Push pretzel sticks into cheese cubes.

3. Put pretzels into holes in apple.

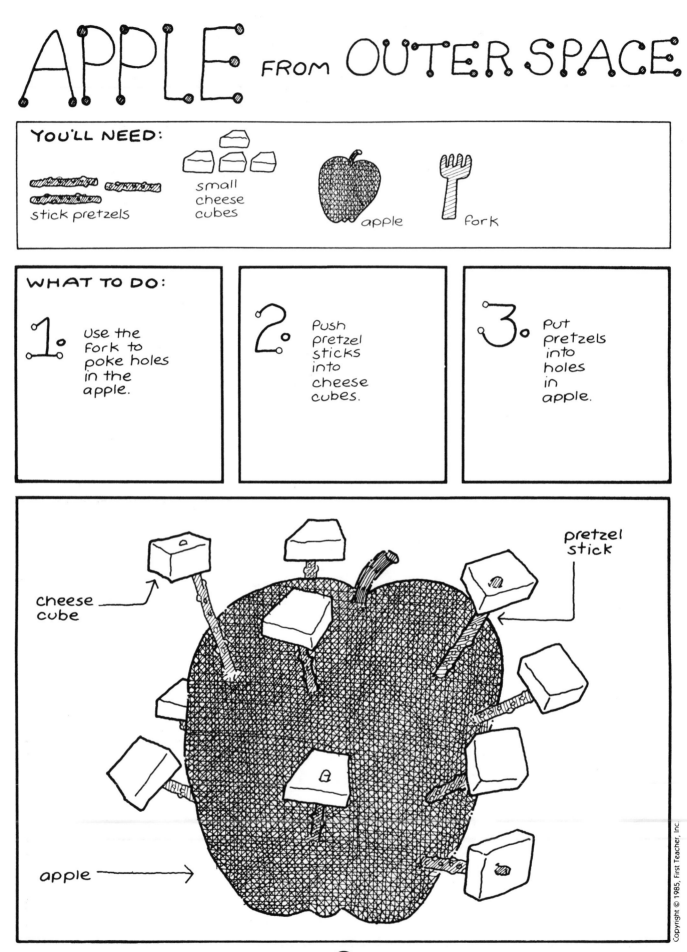

pretzel stick

cheese cube

apple →

YOU'LL NEED:

green pepper

radishes

raisins

cucumbers (peeled)

cherry tomatoes

celery sticks

cream cheese

peanut butter

toothpicks

plastic knife

peanut butter

celery stick

toothpicks

cherry tomato "wheels"

green pepper wedge filled with cream cheese and raisins

cucumber slice "wheel"

toothpick

WHAT TO DO:

1. Wash and use plastic knife to cut vegetables as follows: radishes into slices; cucumbers into slices and wedges; green pepper into wedges.

radish

cucumber slice

cucumber wedge

green pepper wedge

2. Spread cucumber wedge with cream cheese. Fill green pepper wedge with cream cheese. Fill celery stick with peanut butter.

3. Attach radish and cucumber slice "wheels" with toothpicks. Use cherry tomatoes as wheels, also.

4. Decorate with raisins and more vegetables.

Cucumber wedge with cream cheese

toothpick

cucumber slice

CORN DOGGIES

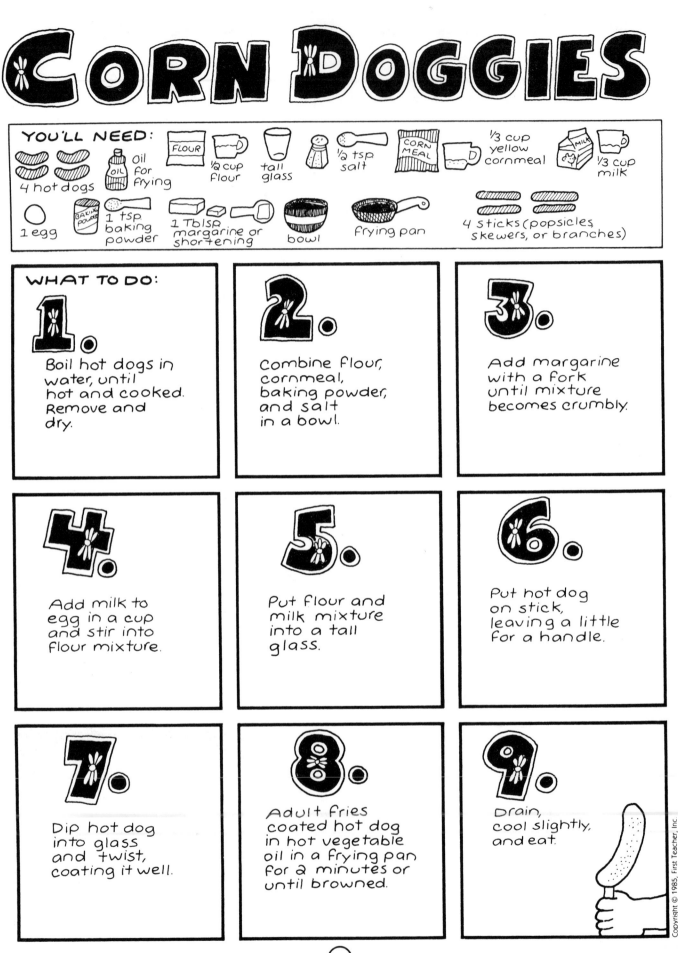

YOU'LL NEED:

4 hot dogs · Oil for frying · ½ cup flour · tall glass · ½ tsp salt · CORN MEAL · ⅓ cup yellow cornmeal · ⅓ cup milk

1 egg · 1 tsp. baking powder · 1 Tblsp. margarine or shortening · bowl · frying pan · 4 sticks (popsicles, skewers, or branches)

WHAT TO DO:

1. Boil hot dogs in water, until hot and cooked. Remove and dry.

2. Combine flour, cornmeal, baking powder, and salt in a bowl.

3. Add margarine with a fork until mixture becomes crumbly.

4. Add milk to egg in a cup and stir into flour mixture.

5. Put flour and milk mixture into a tall glass.

6. Put hot dog on stick, leaving a little for a handle.

7. Dip hot dog into glass and twist, coating it well.

8. Adult fries coated hot dog in hot vegetable oil in a frying pan for 2 minutes or until browned.

9. Drain, cool slightly, and eat.

PIGS IN BLANKETS

YOU'LL NEED:

4 frankfurters

2 cups biscuit mix

2/3 cup milk

baking sheet

biscuit mix covered board

knife (ADULT USE ONLY)

WHAT TO DO:

1. Adult cuts frankfurters in half lengthwise.

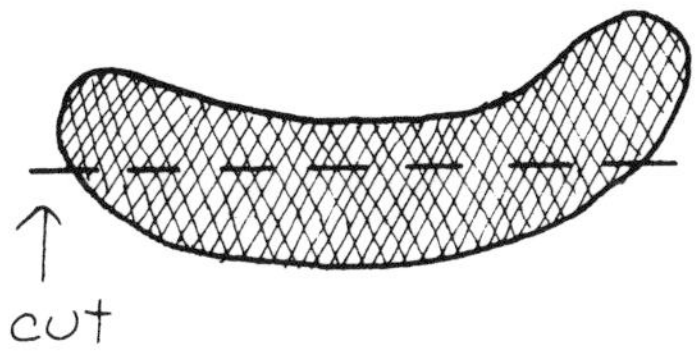

cut

2. Mix biscuit mix with milk. knead 10 times on a biscuit mix-covered board. Dough should be stiff.

3. Divide dough into 8 parts. Roll each into a snake shape (about 8"). Flatten slightly.

snake shape dough

biscuit mix powder

4. wrap dough around frankfurter half. Moisten dough edges to keep them together.

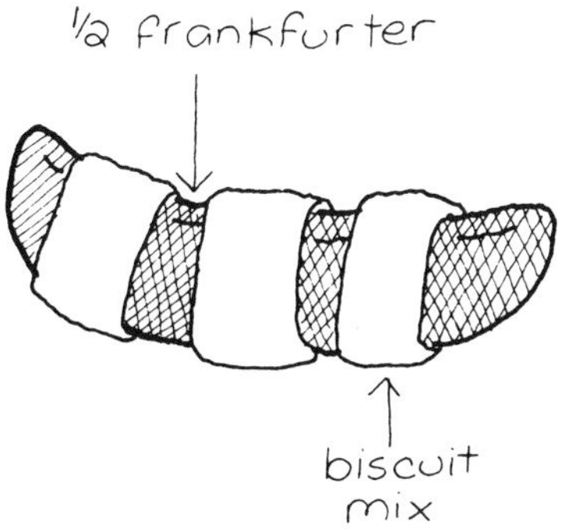

½ frankfurter

biscuit mix

5. Place on an ungreased baking sheet. Bake at 450°F for 10 minutes.

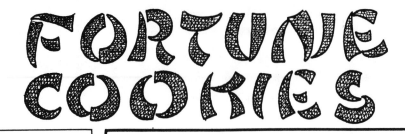

FORTUNE COOKIES

YOU'LL NEED:

1/3 cup flour

FLOUR

1 1/2 Tblsp. corn starch

CORN STARCH

2 Tblsp. oil

OIL

dash salt

1/4 tsp. vanilla

cup

1 egg white-beaten stiff

oven mitt

4 Tblsp. water

BROWN SUGAR

2 Tblsp. brown sugar

non-stick skillet

empty egg carton

bowls

mixing spoon

8 paper strips with silly riddles and answers on them.

WHAT TO DO:

1. combine flour, sugar, salt, and cornstarch.

2. Mix oil and egg white. Add to flour mix.

3. Add water and vanilla. Mix well.

4. Pour 1 heaping Tblsp. of batter on a non-stick skillet, using medium heat. Spread into a 3" circle.

5. Cook 4 minutes until brown. Turn and cook 2 minutes on other side.

6. Remove from pan. Place riddle strip on circle. Use oven mitt to fold circle in half, pressing firmly. Bend folded side over rim of a cup. (See Diagrams A and B.)

7. Cool in an empty egg carton. (see Diagram C.)

8. Crisp cookies in a 350°F oven for 10 minutes.

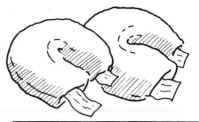

A

SAMPLE FORTUNE COOKIE RIDDLE STRIPS

Why did the robber take a bath?

He wanted to make a clean get-away.

What do you have if you put a mother duck and her ducklings in a box?

A box of quackers.

Why does the fireman wear red suspenders?

To keep his pants from falling down.

What time is it when an elephants sits on your fence?

Time to get a new fence.

B

HOW TO FOLD FORTUNE COOKIES

① ← riddle strip
← cooked batter

② fold

③ fold
← cup

④

A FORTUNE COOKIE!

C

HOW TO COOL FORTUNE COOKIES

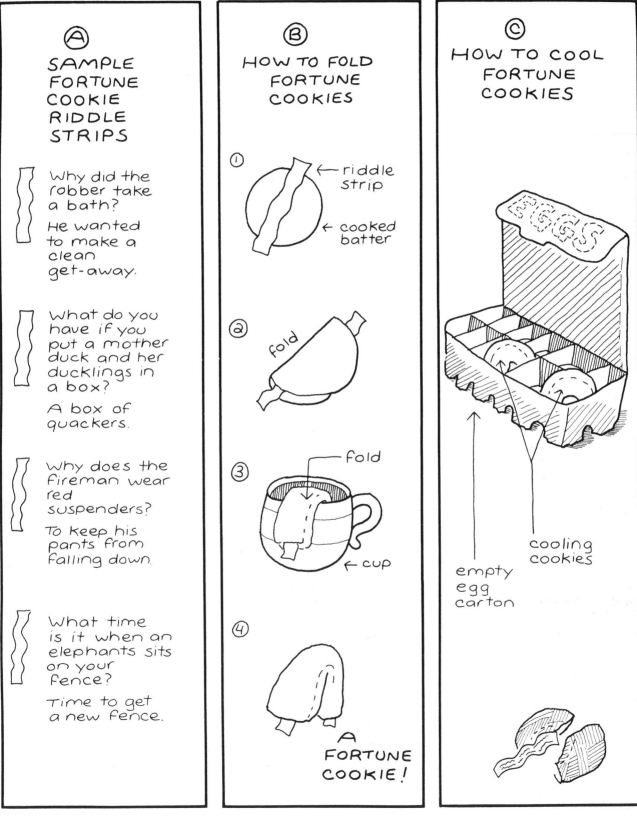

EGGS

cooling cookies

empty egg carton

NOTES

NOTES

RECIPES

RECIPES

RECIPES

RECIPES